IN THE
CARE OF
THE STATE?

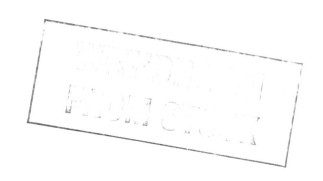

IN THE CARE OF THE STATE?
Child Deaths in Penal Custody in England and Wales

Barry Goldson and Deborah Coles

Working for truth, justice and accountability

British Library Cataloguing in Publication Data
A catalogue record for this book is available from the British Library

ISBN 0 9468 5819 5

First published in 2005 by:

INQUEST
Working for truth, justice and accountability
89-93 Fonthill Road, London N4 3JH, UK
Tel: 020 7263 1111 Fax: 020 7561 0799
Email: inquest@inquest.org.uk
Website: www.inquest.org.uk

Cover design and layout by:
smith+bell (smithplusbell@aol.com)

Printed by:
Russell Press, Nottingham (info@russellpress.com)

Dedication

This book is dedicated to the memory of the 28 children whose lives were lost to penal custody in England and Wales between July 1990 and January 2005:

Andrew Batey, died August 8 1994, aged 17, HMP Low Newton;
Mark Dade, died July 27 2001, aged 16, HMYOI Wetherby;
David Dennis, died May 30 2000, aged 17, HMYOI Brinsford;
Kirk Edwards, died May 30 1999, aged 17, HMYOI Wetherby;
Chris Greenaway, died October 2 1995, aged 16, HMP Stoke Heath;
Philip Griffin, died August 1 2000, aged 17, HMYOI Wetherby;
Kevin Henson, died September 6 2000, aged 17, HMYOI Feltham;
Jeffrey Horler, died September 22 1991, aged 15, HMYOI Feltham;
Anthony Howarth, died August 29 1999, aged 17, HMYOI Hindley;
Kevin Jacobs, died September 29 2001, aged 16, HMYOI Feltham;
John Keyworth, died November 10 1998, aged 17, HMYOI Hindley;
Philip Knight, died July 12 1990, aged 15, HMP Swansea;
Patrick Murphy, died May 2 1992, aged 16, HMYOI Deerbolt;
Gareth Myatt, died April 19 2004, aged 15, Rainsbrook Secure Training Centre;
Ian Powell, died October 6 2002, aged 17, HMP Parc;
Gareth Price, died January 20 2005, aged 16, HMYOI Lancaster Farms;
Anthony Redding, died February 15 2001, aged 16, HMYOI Brinsford;
Adam Rickwood, died August 9 2004, aged 14, Hassockfield Secure Training Centre;
Colin Scarborough, died April 17 1998, aged 17, HMP Doncaster;
Joseph Scholes, died March 24 2002, aged 16, HMYOI Stoke Heath;
Joseph Stanley, died May 10 1994, aged 17, HMP Cardiff;
David Stewart, died September 13 1993, aged 17, HMP Exeter;
Lee Wagstaff, died January 17 1997, aged 17, HMYOI Hindley;
Craig Walsh, died October 26 1990, aged 15, HMYOI Glen Parva;
Mark Weldrand, died December 3 1995, aged 16, HMP Doncaster;
Nicholas Whelan, died July 9 1998, aged 16, HMYOI Glen Parva;
Simon Willerton, died August 12 1990, aged 17, HMP Leeds;
Ryan Winter, died August 13 1996, aged 17, HMYOI Lewes;

and to all of their bereaved parents, siblings, relatives and friends.

Contents

Preface

This book reports the findings from research into child deaths in penal custody in England and Wales. It is the first detailed and sustained analysis of child deaths to be published in the UK and, as far as we are aware, there are no similar accounts available anywhere else in the world.

Chapter 1 describes the background, the principal objectives and the primary research methods that underpin the book. Chapter 2 traces the key shifts in contemporary youth justice law and policy that have initiated penal expansion and considers the consequences of such developments for child prisoners. Chapter 3 explicitly addresses child deaths in penal custody alongside a critical analysis of the responses to such deaths by key state agencies. Chapter 4 examines the post-death investigation and inquest processes that are activated when a child dies in penal custody. Finally, chapter 5 sets out our key conclusions and recommendations.

As stated, the book is derived from detailed research and a thorough analysis of evidence, together with lessons that have been drawn from substantial practical experience. It is offered as an interventionist text and we truly hope that it succeeds in contributing to progressive change. We have attempted to present complex material in an accessible form and, to help with this, we have included a summary of key issues at the beginning of the book.

We are indebted to many people and it is not practical to list them all here. Some acknowledgements are vital, however.

What follows would not have been possible without the generous funding provided to INQUEST by The Diana, Princess of Wales, Memorial Fund, and for this we are both deeply grateful. The funding enabled INQUEST to commission the University of Liverpool to research child deaths in penal custody as a major part of a wider project that also covers the deaths of young adult prisoners.

We have been assisted, directly and indirectly, by an extremely broad range of people from organisations and agencies including: the Children's Society; the Children's Rights Alliance for England; Her Majesty's Prisons Inspectorate; House of Lords House of Commons Joint Committee on Human Rights; the Home Office; the Howard League for Penal Reform; INQUEST Family Forum;

Liberty; Nacro; the National Association for Youth Justice; the Prison Service; the Prison Reform Trust; the Prisons and Probation Ombudsman's office; Statewatch; the United Families and Friends Campaign and the Youth Justice Board for England and Wales, together with innumerable others from the academic, social research and policy communities.

Staff at INQUEST have been a constant source of support and assistance. In particular the inspiring and enormously important work of the senior caseworker, Gilly Mundy, merits special acknowledgement. Equally, academic and library staff at the University of Liverpool continue to provide the collegiality and expert assistance that helps to make work of this nature possible.

We dedicate the book to the memories of the 28 children who died in penal custody in England and Wales between July 1990 and January 2005, and to their parents, siblings, relatives and friends. We also wish to acknowledge the courage, determination and integrity that is characteristic of many bereaved families following child deaths in penal custody and, in this sense, the contribution that Yvonne Scholes has made in deepening our understanding is extraordinary.

Finally, special thanks to Mark Scott, Phil Scraton, Helen Shaw, Joe Sim and Tony Ward, not only for their long-standing and substantial contributions to the search for truth and justice but, more particularly, for reading and commenting upon draft versions of the manuscript. Their incisive and learned feedback was invaluable although only we are responsible for any omissions or errors.

Barry Goldson and Deborah Coles

Summary of Key Issues

Chapter 1 – In the Care of the State?

■ In May 2005, the total prison population in England and Wales exceeded 76,000 for the first time in penal history. With specific regard to children, greater use of penal custody is made in England and Wales than in most other industrialised democratic countries in the world.

■ Her Majesty's Chief Inspector of Prisons has reported that the prison system is lodged on the cusp of a 'manageable crisis and an unmanageable one'.

■ The rate of self-inflicted deaths within the general prison population continues to run at nearly two a week and there were 17,678 self-harm incidents in one year alone between 2003 and 2004.

■ Throughout the period January 1990 – May 2005 the total number of self-inflicted deaths in prison custody was 1076. For young adult prisoners (aged 18-21) the figure stood at 162 and for child prisoners (aged 10-17), including those held in Secure Training Centres, the total number of deaths was 28.

■ INQUEST has consistently raised concerns in relation to deaths of child and young adult prisoners, together with the frequently negative experiences of families throughout post-death investigation and inquest processes. Despite this child deaths in penal custody have, in many important respects, been neglected.

■ It is difficult to comprehend how 28 children could have died in penal custody in England and Wales between July 1990 and January 2005 without a public inquiry into any of the deaths. Each and all of these children died in the 'care' of the state.

■ Child deaths in penal custody remains a marginal concern for too many people with power and responsibility and, in particular, the government continues to negate its moral and democratic obligations.

■ This book: investigates the structural and institutional conditions that give rise to death, harm and damage with specific regard to children in penal custody; examines in detail child deaths in penal custody between 1990 and 2005; analyses post-death investigations and inquests, with particular emphasis on the experiences of the bereaved. It reaches conclusions and makes recommendations and the consolidating aim is to advance knowledge, activate progressive reform and improve practice.

Chapter 2 – Children in Penal Custody

■ The practice of detaining children in various forms of penal custody is long-established in England and Wales. This suggests that such practices are uncontested and that policy formation has followed a continuous progressive line. In reality, however, youth justice policy processes are characterised by both discontinuities and regressive features.

■ Analysis of policy development from the early 1980s to date illustrates both a lack of coherence and, particularly in recent years, an increasingly punitive thrust.

■ Throughout the 1980s, law and policy provided for the practice of decarceration and served to substantially reduce the number of children held in penal custody.

■ The policy and practice of decarceration was credited, by David Faulkner the Head of the Home Office Crime Department between 1982 and 1990, with the 'visible reduction of known juvenile offending'.

■ In the early 1990s the direction of youth justice policy took a dramatic 'U-turn', signalling a new politics of 'toughness'.

■ The cumulative effect of developments in law and policy from 1994 to the present, has been to provide for the detention of more, and younger, children in penal custody.

■ The contemporary penal trend bears virtually no relation to patterns of youth crime.

■ Statistics indicate that both the incidence and the seriousness of juvenile crime are stable, if not declining. The increase in child prisoners is anomalous, therefore.

■ The punitive intent of contemporary youth justice law and policy is driven more by political calculations than it is by penological rationality.

■ In the early 21st Century the total prison population in England and Wales is proportionately the highest among the countries of the European Union.

■ Between 1994 and 2004, the number of children sentenced to penal custody in England and Wales increased by 90 per cent and the number remanded to penal custody increased by 142 per cent. The length of custodial sentences has also increased significantly.

■ The number of 12-14-year-old children held in penal custody in England and Wales has increased by 800 per cent and the number of girls imprisoned has increased by 500 per cent, over the same ten year period.

■ Racism permeates the youth justice system and black children continue to be substantially over-represented within the population of child prisoners.

■ Research evidence and practice experience confirms that the biographies of child prisoners are routinely disfigured by multiple and intersecting forms of social disadvantage.

■ The 'Juvenile Secure Estate' comprises three different types of institutions: Local Authority Secure Children's Homes (provided and managed by Social Services Departments and the Department for Education and Skills); Secure Training Centres (provided and managed by the private sector under contract to the Home Office); and Young Offender Institutions (provided and managed by the Prison Service and the Home Office). The overwhelming majority of children in penal custody are held in Young Offender Institutions.

■ According to the High Court Judge, Mr Justice Munby, the conditions and treatment of children in Young Offender Institutions 'ought to shock the conscience of every citizen'.

■ The human costs of penal custody for children are immeasurable. The authoritative *Chief Inspectors' Report on Arrangements to Safeguard Children*, published in 2002, observed that child prisoners are profoundly vulnerable and that those in Young Offender Institutions 'face the gravest risk to their welfare'.

■ The fiscal costs of keeping children in penal custody are extremely high. In the financial year 2003-04 alone, £293.5 million was spent for this purpose.

■ The failure of penal custody as a measure of crime prevention is very well documented. Reconviction rates in respect of children following release from all forms of penal custody are exceptionally high.

■ In October 2004, a Parliamentary Select Committee reported that re-conviction rates stand at 80 per cent with regard to child prisoners following release.

■ There is little, if any, rational justification for the policies and practices of penal expansion. Detaining increasing numbers of children in penal custody intensifies the danger, damage and harm that they face; imposes a substantial burden on the Treasury; and ultimately fails to provide a safer society.

■ There is a pressing need for a comprehensive review of such policies and practices.

Chapter 3 – Child Deaths in Penal Custody

■ Between July 1990 and January 2005, 28 children died in penal custody: an average of two child deaths every year, all but two self-inflicted.

■ During the same period of time literally thousands of children harmed themselves in penal custody: 1,659 incidents of self-injury or attempted suicide by children in prisons were recorded from 1998 to 2002. It is more difficult to measure and quantify the less tangible detrimental impact – physical, psychological, emotional hurt – that penal custody inflicts on children, but thousands more have been damaged.

■ Death, harm and damage is not only a permanent feature of penal custody but, with the passage of time, statistics suggest that it has become more commonplace. Despite constant policy reform and practice experimentation towards the goal of 'safer custody', the 'jail-house', however it is configured, remains a dangerous place particularly for children.

■ 'Safer custody' policy and practice can be traced back to the first Prison Service Circular Instruction in 1973.

■ Further Circular Instructions, issued in 1983, proposed the formation of 'management groups' in prisons to develop, co-ordinate and implement suicide prevention policies and practices.

■ Such responses were underpinned by a medical emphasis and this was reinforced by a review led by Her Majesty's Chief Inspector of Prisons published in 1984. The review conceptualised suicide and self-harm primarily as medical issues and placed the principal responsibility for prevention with the Medical Officer.

■ In 1987 revised 'suicide prevention' procedures came into effect in the Prison Service and were soon followed by the publication of a further Circular Instruction on the 'Prevention of Suicide and Self-Injury' in 1989. The Instruction provided for the establishment of a 'Suicide Prevention Management Group' (SPMG) in each prison. Medical Officers were made wholly responsible for assessing risk and defining appropriate responses.

■ In February 1990, the Home Secretary, David Waddington, announced another review to be conducted by Her Majesty's Chief Inspector of Prisons, Sir Stephen Tumin. Tumin's report, published in December 1990, took issue with previous policies, practices and procedures that treated 'self-inflicted death as exclusively a medical problem'.

■ Further to the publication of Sir Stephen Tumin's report, the Prison Service established the 'Suicide Awareness Support Unit' in 1991, dedicated to developing and communicating national strategy, disseminating research and good practice and providing advice and support to local 'Suicide Prevention Management Groups'. A range of policies on suicide awareness and guidance from the Prison Service followed.

■ In December 1997, the Minister for Prisons, Joyce Quinn, asked Sir David Ramsbotham, Her Majesty's Chief Inspector of Prisons, to carry out a thematic review of suicide and self-harm in Prison Service establishments.

In particular, attention was drawn to child and young prisoners whose specific needs and unique circumstances previously had been overlooked.

■ In recent years a Ministerial 'Roundtable' on 'Suicide in Prisons' has convened. Alongside the 'Roundtable', a range of additional measures have been implemented in an effort to minimise the likelihood of death, harm and damage in penal custody.

■ With specific regard to child prisoners, perhaps the single-most significant reform has been the establishment, by the Crime and Disorder Act 1998, of a new executive non-departmental public body, the Youth Justice Board for England and Wales (YJB). The YJB has endeavoured – along with its other duties – to apply the 'safer custody' agenda to the 'juvenile secure estate'. In doing this, particular emphasis has focussed upon questions of placement, assessment and protection.

■ In order to fulfil its 'commissioning' functions and operationalise its 'contracting' arrangements, the YJB – in consultation with the Home Office and the Department of Health – established 'purchasing agreements' with 'placement providers', based upon agreed costings and service specifications and located within a 'comprehensive performance monitoring framework'. Ostensibly this provides rationality within which the YJB is able to 'purchase' 'placements' from the 'providers' (the Prison Service, the Local Authority Secure Children's Homes and the privately managed Secure Training Centres), allowing it to place children in an establishment that can most effectively manage their identified needs and risk factors.

■ In practice 'placements' are ultimately governed by availability, supply and cost and, accordingly, the placements process is determined by pragmatism and expediency as distinct from qualitative welfare-based judgements regarding children's respective needs and risks. The overwhelming majority of 'placements' are located within Young Offender Institutions. It follows that at any one time significant numbers of manifestly vulnerable children are inappropriately 'placed' in prisons.

■ The Prison Service and the YJB have also attempted to minimise the likelihood of child deaths, harm and damage in penal custody by developing more detailed 'assessment' policies, practices and procedures. Since its inception the YJB has emphasised consistently the importance of continuous or 'joined-up' assessment for children sent to penal custody. The process of assessment that has developed involves contributions from various agencies and, in its complete form, it comprises at least seven discrete but inter-connected stages, each of which is (in theory) accompanied by specific documentation.

■ In practice the assessment processes 'haemorrhage' significant quantities of crucially relevant information. Furthermore, the 'assessments' that are applied in Young Offender Institutions are institutionally expedient, hasty and cursory.

■ Child protection policies have also developed. Prison Service Order 4950 'Regimes for Under 18 year Olds', was revised in 2003 to include a detailed sequence of 'annexes' and 'appendices' setting out child protection law, guidance, policy, procedure, process and practice, together with a range of pro-forma documents for the purposes of executing and recording child protection interventions in penal custody.

■ Also in 2003, Her Majesty's Prison Service 'Juvenile Group', in partnership with the Youth Justice Board for England and Wales, implemented a 'Child Protection and Safeguards Review'.

■ In 2004, the Department for Education and Skills issued a Local Authority Circular entitled 'Safeguarding and promoting the welfare of children and young people in custody'. The same year the Youth Justice Board for England and Wales issued a three-year 'Strategy for the Secure Estate for Juveniles' in which it set out its determination to 'ensure that young offenders are cared for in custodial establishments where they are kept safe and healthy in decent conditions'.

■ In practice, despite the various developments with regard to child protection policies and procedures, Her Majesty's Chief Inspector of Prisons reported in 2005 that progress is 'patchy'

■ Paradoxically, the consolidation and development of the 'safer custody' agenda has been accompanied by record levels of self-inflicted deaths and individual and collective harm and damage.

■ The tensions between punitive policies and practices that ultimately serve to increase the use of penal custody for children on the one hand, and more benign responses that aim to take account of children's individual needs on the other, are apparent. Such tensions impose enormous pressure upon the 'juvenile secure estate'.

■ The concept of 'safer custody' or the 'caring prison' is, in essence, an oxymoron. There is little or no evidence to imply that the innumerable policies, practices and procedures designed to provide safe environments for children in penal custody have succeeded.

■ The depressing reality, given the increasing use of penal custody for children, is that more death, harm and damage is certain to follow.

Chapter 4 – Post-Death Investigations and Inquests

■ Child deaths in penal custody are important matters of public concern.

■ When a child dies in penal custody the state must be presumed to have failed in its 'duty of care'

■ To be informed that a child has died in penal custody can only be devastating for their immediate family. The evidence is that some families have been informed of such deaths in ways that were highly insensitive, many have been given insufficient information about what had happened, some have been given inaccurate information and several have been obstructed in their attempts to obtain further information.

■ The need for a thorough investigation following a child's death in penal custody is self-evident. Any fault in the system for protecting the right to life could very well lead to another loss of life. The state also fails, therefore, if it does not investigate such deaths properly.

■ In cases where a child's death is self-inflicted and the police are satisfied that there are no grounds for prosecution, at least two separate but related processes are conventionally activated. First, the penal institution will commence its own *investigation*. Second, the Coroner's Court will be notified and the Coroner will ultimately preside over an *inquest*.

■ In 1998 Her Majesty's Prison Service issued guidance and instructions on investigation procedures to be followed after a death in custody. Prison Service Order 2710 set out the key stages of the investigatory process. At the time of writing, a revised Prison Service Order 2710 ('Follow up to deaths in custody') has been drafted but publication has not yet been authorised and no implementation date has been fixed.

■ Inquests are governed by the Coroners Act (CA) 1988 and the Coroners Rules (CR) 1984. Section 8 of the CA 1988 requires that any inquest into the death of a person in prison must always be held before a jury and Rule 17 of the CR 1984 stipulates that such inquests must also be held in public.

■ The CA 1988 (s. 11) and CR 1984 (r. 36) also provide that proceedings and evidence at an inquest should be directed exclusively towards addressing four key questions: *who* the deceased was; *where* the deceased came by their death; *when* the deceased came by their death; and *how* the deceased came by their death.

■ Inquests are statutorily defined as *inquisitorial* 'fact finding' exercises as distinct from *adversarial* processes designed to apportion responsibility, liability, blame and/or guilt.

■ The system of investigations and inquests might appear to provide for comprehensive scrutiny in order that both the specific and more general circumstances of child deaths in penal custody may be fully examined. The investigatory and inquest apparatus is surrounded by controversy, however, and it has attracted substantial critical attention in recent years that has served to initiate, at least in part, statutory reform.

■ With regard to investigations, questions relating to the *disclosure of information* and the *independence* of investigatory processes have given particular cause for concern. Up until April 1999, the policy of the Prison Service was to treat the reports of investigations into deaths in custody as confidential documents and, as such, they were not available for routine disclosure. Furthermore, the Prison Service effectively investigated itself in such cases. Such arrangements failed to instil public confidence.

■ Since April 2004, the investigatory function has been transferred from the Prison Service to the Prisons and Probation Ombudsman. The Ombudsman issued 'guidance on disclosure' in March 2005. This guidance is welcome but it falls short of granting unconditional disclosure and it lacks a firm statutory footing.

■ Whilst such reform may be taken to signal progress, it fails in establishing a truly independent investigatory system. Disclosure remains conditional, the Ombudsman's investigatory function is exercised on a non-statutory basis and the office has no power to compel the production of evidence.

■ In relation to inquests the narrow confines within which they operate are, in effect, prohibitive: they can serve to conceal more than they reveal in respect of the broader circumstances within which child deaths in penal custody are located. Not unlike the position with investigations, such critique, at least in part, has prompted recent reform.

■ In July 2001 the Home Office established a 'Fundamental Review of Death Certification and Coroner Services' and the review team reported in June 2003, offering 123 recommendations covering organisation, resources, procedure verdicts and family rights.

■ The government's response to the 'Fundamental Review', published in 2004, signalled some support for its recommendations and stated that a White Paper and draft Bill on reform of the inquest system would be published in Spring 2005. Although at the time of writing, neither the White Paper nor the draft Bill have yet been published, 'reform of the coroner's system' was announced in the Queen's Speech on 17 May, 2005 and a Coroner Reform Bill is listed in the 2005/06 schedule of Parliamentary Business. Furthermore, responsibility for Coroners was passed from the Home Office to the Department of Constitutional Affairs on June 1 2005.

■ The European Convention on Human Rights and the Human Rights Act 1998 are also significant in the drive for reforming post-death investigations and inquests.

■ Article 2 of the European Convention on Human Rights (ECHR), the 'Right to Life', is taken to be the most fundamental of human rights. More specifically, the right has also been identified as extending to taking positive steps to prevent self-inflicted deaths in penal custody and, further still, this requires an 'effective investigation' where death has occurred in a way that engages with the provisions of the Convention. The lack of an *effective investigation* can in itself be taken to constitute a violation of Article 2.

■ The procedural obligation that arises under Article 2, to conduct an 'effective investigation', has obvious implications for investigations and inquests following child deaths in penal custody. In accordance with the European Convention on Human Rights and the Human Rights Act 1998, therefore, it is reasonable to conclude that investigations and inquests in respect of these deaths should be underpinned by, and/or facilitate the application of, five sets of inter-related principles. First, *state instigation* and yet *independence* of investigation. Second, *effectiveness* and unfettered *disclosure* of all relevant documentation. Third, *promptness* and *reasonable expedition*. Fourth, *transparency* and *integrity*. Fifth, *family participation*. Such principles, offer a 'benchmarking' framework within which current policy and practice can be critically assessed.

■ By rigorously applying the five sets of intersecting 'benchmarking' principles, by examining the relevant documentation and research evidence and by taking direct account of the experiences of bereaved families and those who work most closely with them, it is difficult to avoid the conclusion that the system continues to produce and reproduce failure.

■ The limited independence and effectiveness of investigation and inquest processes, their circumscribed scope, the ongoing impediments to disclosure and transparency and protracted bureaucratic proceedings all combine to seriously impede family participation.

■ Investigations and inquests following child deaths in penal custody simply do not allow for a thorough, full and fearless inquiry, for discussion of the wider policy issues, or for accountability of those responsible at an individual and institutional level. Neither do they necessarily facilitate an honest and open approach that might help to ensure that changes are made to prevent future child deaths in similar circumstances.

■ In practice investigations and inquests sustain a culture of defensiveness and institutional protection. The fundamental rights of bereaved families are not properly respected and the agencies and institutions of the state and, in the case of Secure Training Centres, private agencies and institutions with which the state 'does business', are insufficiently scrutinised when children die in their 'care'. In the final analysis, the system continues to obfuscate truth, limit accountability and deny justice.

Chapter 5 – Key Conclusions and Recommendations

■ Numerous conclusions and recommendations are contained within the body of this book, some implicit within the overall analysis and others are more explicitly stated. It is not the intention, however, to produce an extended list of 'micro' recommendations, not least because such lists have been expertly presented elsewhere.

■ Given that this book comprises the first detailed analysis of child deaths in penal custody in England and Wales, however, it would not be possible to end without providing some key conclusions and 'macro' recommendations. Thus, four sets of related and overlapping conclusions and recommendations are offered that, taken together, distil the underpinning messages of the book.

■ Our first conclusion is that despite the various policy and procedural reforms that have been, and continue to be, implemented, and the practical efforts of some operational staff to take account of the specific needs of child prisoners, penal custody remains an unsuitable environment for children. 'Caring' for children in penal custody, especially Young Offender Institutions, is an almost impossible task. Many child prisoners live with a spectre of fear and an enduring feeling of being 'unsafe'. This, in turn, is thought to heighten the risk of damage and/or death: what one leading academic commentator has termed an 'invitation to suicide'.

■ Our first recommendation, therefore, is the abolition of all Prison Service and Private Sector custody for child 'offenders', and only the minimum use of Local Authority Secure Children's Home provision for children whose behaviour places themselves and/or others at demonstrable serious risk. In cases where children are deprived of their liberty 'as a measure of last resort and for the shortest appropriate period of time', the full weight of all relevant international human/children's rights standards, treaties, rules and conventions should, of necessity, apply as minimum and non-negotiable safeguards.

■ Our second conclusion is that the question of 'how' an individual child came by their death in penal custody, the primary preoccupation of investigations and inquests, is by definition circumscribed. It is essentially confined to an individual child in a given penal institution at a specific moment in time. It is necessarily abstracted from analysis of youth justice policy and/or any consideration of the wider social, structural, material and institutional arrangements that defined the child's circumstances prior to death. If such deliberate and institutionalised circumscription obscures understanding of individual cases of child deaths in penal custody, it also completely negates the combined and/or collective lessons that might otherwise be drawn from an aggregated understanding of multiple cases. It follows, that the lessons that might be learned from such an analysis, together with the benefits that could ensue from their application, continue to elude.

■ Our second recommendation, therefore, is that measures should be implemented to: investigate the policy contexts and commonalities of circumstance that characterise child deaths in penal custody by means of a comprehensive and thorough review; learn and apply the lessons gleaned from such a review; routinely publish recommendations from individual inquests and systematically monitor the implementation of the same. The formation of an *independent* body will be necessary in order to facilitate the implementation of such measures.

■ Our third conclusion is that a robust independent body, a 'Standing Commission', is necessary in order to systematically address the question of deaths in custody in general and child deaths in particular. There are many common concerns that link individual child deaths together, just as there are issues that transcend the narrowly focussed remits of specific government departments and state agencies. A 'Standing Commission on Custodial Deaths' would serve to look beyond individual cases and/or particular state agencies and engage with child deaths in penal custody on a more holistic and collective basis.

■ Our third recommendation, therefore, is that a 'Standing Commission on Custodial Deaths' should be established to collect, collate, analyse and publish findings in respect of child deaths, identify common issues, develop programmes of research and, pending the abolition of the use of Prison Service and Private Sector custody for children, assist in the development and delivery of 'best practice' in safeguarding children and promoting a 'duty of care' towards them. We would expect the 'Standing Commission' to be statutorily empowered to intervene in individual inquests where appropriate as an 'interested party'. Indeed, we envisage an active interventionist role for the 'Commission', underpinned by the power to hold a wider inquiry and to summon witnesses in circumstances where there might be a consistent pattern of deaths, as in the case of child deaths in penal custody.

■ Our fourth conclusion relates to the death of Joseph Scholes. Joseph hanged himself from the bars of his cell in Stoke Heath Young Offenders Institution on March 24, 2002. In November 2003 Joseph's mother, Yvonne Scholes, together with INQUEST and Nacro (a national 'crime reduction agency') launched a call in the House of Commons for a public inquiry into his death. The call was almost immediately supported by over 100 MPs and Peers, many other individuals in public life and a wide range of penal reform, child welfare and human rights organisations and agencies. Since then, the call has been further and additionally supported by the Coroner who presided over the inquest into Joseph's death, by MPs and Peers in both Houses of Parliament, by officials from the General Synod of the Church of England, and from the House of Lords House of Commons Joint Committee on Human Rights. Despite all of this, however, the Government has consistently refused to allow a public inquiry.

■ Our fourth and final recommendation reiterates the call for a full public inquiry into the circumstances that led to the death of Joseph Scholes. The Government's resistance to this call runs counter to the spirit of democratic accountability, transparency and the pressing need to learn from the failure in the system that cost a 16-year-old child his life. We recommend as a matter of urgency, therefore, that the Government should re-consider its decision and implement a comprehensive public inquiry.

Chapter 1
In the Care of the State?

'We announced our inquiry into human rights and deaths in custody in July 2003... We hope to publish our final report and conclusions on this inquiry in the later part of 2004'. (House of Lords House of Commons Joint Committee on Human Rights, 2004a, paras. 1 and 7)

'The Prison Service has placed a great deal of emphasis in recent years on trying to reduce deaths in custody. When he was Director General of the Prison Service Martin Narey... announced that preventing deaths in custody was his top priority'. (House of Lords House of Commons Joint Committee on Human Rights, 2004b, para 69)

'Deaths in custody of children and young people are especially distressing, and we therefore highlight them for specific comment... there have been some deeply worrying cases of children and young people who have died while *in the care of the state*'. (House of Lords House of Commons Joint Committee on Human Rights, 2004b, para. 73, emphasis added)

'The Government does not accept that the prison system is... unable to meet its duty of care to prisoners'. (House of Lords House of Commons Joint Committee on Human Rights, 2005, para. 120)

Background and context

The above statements represent the tensions, paradoxes and even contradictions that surround the complex and controversial question of deaths in custody. On one hand, in recent years the matter has attracted significant attention from state agencies and some of their most senior officials have publicly expressed a determination to address it. On the other hand, deaths in custody continue to occur with distressing regularity, yet the Government refuses to accept that the penal system is failing to discharge its duty of care to an ever increasing population of prisoners.

Since the early 1990s, the total prison population in England and Wales has expanded significantly and in May 2005 it exceeded 76,000 for the first time in penal history (British Broadcasting Corporation, 2005). A 'new punitiveness' (Goldson, 2002a; Pratt *et al*, 2005) has consolidated and, with specific regard to children,[1] greater use of penal custody[2] is made in England and Wales than in most other industrialised democratic countries in the world (Youth Justice Board, 2004a, para. 9). Her Majesty's Chief Inspector of Prisons (2005) has reported that the prison system is 24 per cent overcrowded; lodged on the cusp of a 'manageable crisis and an unmanageable one' (*ibid*, p. 7).

This 'crisis', precipitated by substantial penal expansion and endemic overcrowding, is corrosive; it seriously undermines prisoner safety and care (House of Lords House of Commons Joint Committee on Human Rights, 2004b, para. 102-107). This is illustrated clearly by statistical evidence. The rate of self-inflicted deaths within the general prison population 'continues to run at nearly two a week' representing 'the tip of an iceberg of distress' (Her Majesty's Chief Inspector of Prisons, 2005, p.16). In addition to deaths in custody: '228 prisoners were resuscitated and there were 17,678 self-harm incidents' in one year alone between 2003 and 2004 (*ibid*, p. 16). Moreover, as detailed in chapter 3, deaths in penal custody have essentially remained constant over time despite the implementation of a wide range of reforms, 'safer custody' policies, practices and procedures and the best efforts of some staff. Systematic monitoring of deaths in prisons throughout the period January 1990 – May 2005 for example, reveals that the total number of self-inflicted deaths was 1076. For young adult prisoners (aged 18-21) the figure stood at 162 and for child prisoners (aged 10-17), including those held in Secure Training Centres, the total number of deaths was 28 (INQUEST, 2005a).

---

1. The terms 'child' and 'children' are taken to refer to any 'human being below the age of eighteen years' in accordance with Article 1 of the United Nations Convention on the Rights of the Child (United Nations General Assembly, 1989), and section 105 (1) of the Children Act 1989. 'Children in penal custody', however, refers to 10-17 year olds only, otherwise known as 'juveniles'. Once children reach the age of 10 they are held to be fully responsible in criminal proceedings in England and Wales, whereas 17 year old children are treated as 'adults' in criminal law.
2. With regard to child prisoners in England and Wales, the term 'penal custody' applies to three different types of locked institution: Young Offender Institutions provided by the Prison Service; Secure Training Centres provided by the private sector and Local Authority Secure Children's Homes. As detailed in chapters 2 and 3, the overwhelming majority of child prisoners are detained in Prison Service custody and all but two of the child deaths considered in this book have occurred in Young Offender Institutions. Whilst 'penal custody' has a generic application, therefore, in most cases here it can be taken to mean Prison Service custody.

In monitoring deaths in custody in this way and, more significantly, in working directly with bereaved families, INQUEST has consistently raised concerns in relation to deaths of child and young adult prisoners, together with the frequently negative experiences of families throughout post-death investigation and inquest processes. On the basis of contributing to a greater understanding of such complex issues and, in developing its unique and pioneering work with the families of children and young adults who die in penal custody, INQUEST secured funding for an innovative research project. Although the project is addressing both child and young adult deaths, particular emphasis has been placed on the former through a partnership with the University of Liverpool. There is good reason for this, not least because child deaths in penal custody have, in many important respects, been neglected.

On one level, it is difficult to comprehend how 28 children could have died in penal custody in England and Wales between July 1990 and January 2005 without a public inquiry into any of the deaths. Each and all of these children died in the 'care' of the state. Indeed, it might even be argued that they each 'belonged' to the state at the time of their deaths. Yet not a single public inquiry and, in most cases, little more than a murmur of public debate and media interest. This is fundamentally at odds with some notable responses from state and media agencies to child deaths in different, but related, circumstances. Although it has been argued that there was 'a sharp decline in the volume of media coverage of child deaths where the person responsible is a family member between the 1980s and 2000' (Glasgow Media Group, 2001), a number of such cases continue to make high profile news. More significantly, in a multitude of cases where children known to state welfare agencies have died, there have been detailed public inquiries accompanied by sustained public interest and media attention (Corby *et al*, 2001). Similarly, there have been several major public inquiries into the maltreatment, violation and abuse of children in residential settings (see Kahan, 1994), but nothing remotely comparable with regard to children detained in custodial facilities. This is even more perplexing given the adverse personal histories of many child prisoners, their experience of abuse and welfare neglect and the frequent production and reproduction of similar 'treatment' within penal institutions themselves (Goldson, 2000 and 2002b; Stuart and Baines, 2004).

On a 'different level, however, the relative indifference to child deaths in penal custody is less difficult to understand. 'Anti-social' children – whatever that is taken to mean – child 'offenders' and child prisoners in particular, have been cast as 'undeserving' within a socio-political context in England and Wales increasingly characterised by 'institutionalised intolerance' (Muncie, 1999). This process, the political management of child identities, means that identifiable groups of children – none more than child prisoners – are conceptualised primarily as 'threats' requiring control, regulation and even punishment as distinct from 'victims' in need of care, support and welfare assistance (Goldson, 2004a). It follows that some children are seemingly subjected to 'conceptual eviction' and 'removed from the category of "child" altogether' (Jenks, 1996, p. 128). In the final analysis, 'their deaths, and the responsibility for them, are [regarded as being] of lesser significance' (Scraton and Chadwick, 1987a, p.233). As INQUEST has stated:

> 'The failure of the state to act over these appalling deaths suggests that the victims are worthless and sends a clear message that these deaths don't matter'. (INQUEST, cited in Thomas et al, 2002, p. 327)

In this way, child deaths in penal custody, to paraphrase Cohen (2001, p. 1), are 'denied', 'evaded, neutralised or rationalised away'.

Within this overarching context of 'denial', the issue of child deaths in penal custody is, paradoxically, obtaining more significant public exposure at present. This is largely due to the steadfast campaigning of INQUEST together with a range of penal reform organisations, child welfare and children's rights agencies, and, perhaps most significantly, bereaved families. (See for example, INQUEST and Nacro, 2003 and 2004). Despite this, however, child deaths in penal custody remains a marginal concern for too many people with power and responsibility and, in particular, as we argue in chapter 5, the government continues to negate its moral and democratic obligations.

The research that underpins this book, and the publication of the book itself, is timely therefore. We hope that it might contribute to a discernible momentum that is serving to expose: the problematic consequences of penal expansion; the appalling tragedy of 28 child deaths; the inadequate nature of post-death investigations and inquests and the compelling need to take serious action of the form identified throughout the text.

Principal objectives

Four principal objectives have shaped the research design and informed the key questions that underpin the book:

- To investigate the structural and institutional conditions that give rise to death, harm and damage with specific regard to children in penal custody and to offer conclusions and recommendations that might serve to minimise, if not avoid, the same.

- To examine, in detail, child deaths in penal custody between 1990 and 2005 alongside a rigorous critical assessment of penal procedures, policies and practices and to reach conclusions and offer relevant recommendations.
- To analyse post-death investigations and inquests, with particular emphasis on the experiences of the bereaved, and to reach conclusions and make recommendations to promote more effective procedures, policies and practices.
- To present inevitably complex material as accessibly as possible.

In sum, our consolidating aim is to advance knowledge, activate progressive reform and improve practice.

Primary methods

There is no natural 'template' for research of this nature, not least because what follows comprises the first ever detailed analysis of child deaths in penal custody. If the research questions are unique however, the methodological design is relatively conventional. It comprises four complementary dimensions:

- A detailed literature search and documentary analysis drawing upon, and critically assessing, a wide range of source material.
- Case file analyses primarily based upon INQUEST's records from direct casework with the families of children who died in penal custody. Eight case summaries are presented in chapter 3, and these profile children from families with whom INQUEST caseworkers have worked over the years. This was the primary criterion used for selecting cases. Secondary criteria included the need to feature cases that extended over the period of time in question (1990-2005) and together represented the core commonalities that characterise child deaths in penal custody.
- Interviews with bereaved families particularly focussing upon their experiences of post-death investigations and inquests. Whilst we have drawn upon some of this material here a more detailed account will be published in late 2005 (Coles and Shaw, forthcoming, 2005).
- Observations of inquests. We have both attended and observed inquests relating to the deaths of children in penal custody.

In addition to the above, we have each drawn from our combined knowledge and experience of theory, law, policy and practice regarding: youth justice; penal reform; human rights; child welfare; prisons and other locked institutions; contentious deaths and their investigation; the treatment of bereaved people and state accountability.

Chapter 2
Children in Penal Custody

'... no child shall be subjected to... cruel, inhuman or degrading treatment... imprisonment of a child shall be... used only as a measure of last resort and for the shortest appropriate period of time... every child deprived of liberty shall be treated with humanity and respect for the inherent dignity of the human person'. (United Nations General Assembly, 1989, Article 37)

'The chaos that surrounds the treatment of children... in custody leads me to the conclusion that separate arrangements... are essential... From this review, and from inspection of establishments, I am convinced... that children should no longer be its [the Prison Service's] responsibility'. (Her Majesty's Chief Inspector of Prisons, 1997, p. 70)

Introduction

The practice of placing children in penal custody is long-established in England and Wales. Since the creation of the first penal institution exclusively for children at Parkhurst Prison for Boys in 1838, legislation has provided for the penal detention of children in a variety of 'specialist' institutions. The Youthful Offenders Act 1854 sanctioned the 'Reformatory'; the Industrial Schools Act 1857 introduced the 'Industrial School'; the Prevention of Crime Act 1908 ushered in 'Borstals'; the Children and Young Persons Act 1933 served to replace the Reformatory and the Industrial School with the 'Approved School'; the Criminal Justice Act 1948 established 'Remand Centres' and 'Detention Centres'; the Children and Young Persons Act 1969 substituted Approved Schools with 'Community Homes with Education'; the Criminal Justice Act 1982 set up 'Youth Custody Centres'; the Criminal Justice Act 1988 replaced both the Detention and Youth Custody Centres with 'Young Offender Institutions'; the Criminal Justice and Public Order Act 1994 prefaced the opening of 'Secure Training Centres' and, most recently, the Crime and

Disorder Act 1998 has served to 'modernise' what we now have seemingly learnt to call the 'Juvenile Secure Estate' (for a fuller discussion see Goldson, 2002a; Goldson, 2004a; Hagell and Hazel, 2001).

However, such a schematic overview veils the inevitable complexities and controversies that have characterised developments in law, policy and penal practice in England and Wales over the previous two centuries. It also suggests that policy formation follows a continuous progressive line and, in this sense, it masks both the discontinuities and the regressive features of such processes. Analysis of policy development from the early 1980s to date, for example, illustrates both a lack of coherence and, particularly in recent years, an increasingly punitive thrust.

Law and policy 1982-1991: penal reduction

'... most young offenders grow out of crime as they become more mature and responsible. They need encouragement and help to become law-abiding. Even a short period of custody is quite likely to confirm them as criminals, particularly as they acquire new criminal skills from more sophisticated offenders. They see themselves labelled as criminals and behave accordingly'. (Home Office, 1988, paras. 2.17-2.19)

Throughout the 1980s the developing policy agenda appeared to offer genuine relief to those who shared concerns about the legitimacy and efficacy of imprisoning children. Initially the emphasis was placed on those children detained whilst awaiting trial and/or sentence. The practice of remanding 14-year olds girls in penal custody had been abolished in 1977, and powers to impose penal remands on 15- and 16-year old girls and 14-year old boys were similarly removed in 1979 and 1981 respectively (Penal Affairs Consortium, 1996). Furthermore, in its 1981 report – 'Young Offenders: A Strategy for the Future' – the Parliamentary All-Party Penal Affairs Group, recommended that 'a specific timetable should be announced for ending the remand of [all] 15- and 16-year olds in Prison Department establishments and rapid progress should be made towards this objective' (cited in Nacro, 1991). Similarly, in 1984 the Conservative Home Secretary, Leon Brittan, stated that 'the government remains committed to... phasing out the remand to Prison Department establishments of unconvicted or unsentenced juveniles' (cited in Nacro, 1988, p. 4).

The policy of reducing the use of penal custody for children was not only confined to remands, however; it also applied to the practice of custodial sentencing. In 1988, therefore, Virginia Bottomley, a senior Minister in the

Conservative government, reported: 'if anything I have become firmer in my belief that penal custody remains a profoundly unsatisfactory outcome for children' (cited in the Children's Society Advisory Committee on Juvenile Custody and its Alternatives, 1993, p. 18). Throughout the 1980s, law and policy served increasingly to divert children from the criminal justice system in general (the practice of diversion), and to reduce their detention in penal custody in particular (the practice of decarceration):

- The Criminal Justice Act 1982 introduced 'criteria for custody' which served to impose restrictions on the courts' powers to impose custodial sentences. The Act also replaced the indeterminate 'Borstal Training Order' with the determinate disposal of 'Youth Custody' and it further introduced the 'Specified Activities Order' as a direct alternative to penal custody.
- In 1983, partly in response to the 'specified activity' provisions of the 1982 Act, the Department of Health and Social Security, made £15 million available in order to support the development of alternative to custody projects. 110 such projects were established by voluntary organisations in partnership with 62 local authority Social Services Departments in England and Wales.
- Official circulars in 1985 (Home Office, 1985) and 1990 (Home Office, 1990) supported the development of cautioning initiatives in order to divert children from the formal criminal justice process.
- The Prosecution of Offences Act 1985 established the Crown Prosecution Service to provide all areas of England and Wales with a specialist Crown Prosecutor for juveniles. Moreover, the Code for Crown Prosecutors specified that children should only be prosecuted as a 'last resort' and when it was clearly in the public interest.
- The Criminal Justice Act 1988 tightened the criteria for custody further and created a unified sentence of detention in a Young Offender Institution to replace the separate disposals of Detention Centre and Youth Custody.
- The Children Act 1989 established that 'the welfare of the child is the court's paramount concern' and placed duties on local authorities to make arrangements for the diversion from prosecution of child 'offenders'.
- The Criminal Justice Act 1991 tightened the criteria for custody further still, abolished the sentence of detention in a Young Offender Institution for 14 year old boys and contained provisions, to be implemented at a future time, for the similar abolition of penal remands for all 15-17 year olds.

The combined effect of such developments was not insignificant. By 1990, 70 per cent of boys and 86 per cent of girls aged between 14 and 16 who admitted offences and were accordingly charged, were cautioned and thus diverted from prosecution (Goldson, 1997a, pp.127-128). Similarly, the number of children remanded to penal custody fell from 1630 in 1984 to 1263 in 1990 (Goldson, 2002b, p. 37) and, more significantly still, the number of custodial sentences imposed on children fell from 7900 in 1981 to 1700 in 1990 (Allen, 1991; Goldson, 1997a, p.128). Furthermore, the related policies of diversion and decarceration were effective not only in terms of reducing the number of criminal prosecutions being brought against children and substantially moderating the practice of child imprisonment but also, according to David Faulkner the Head of the Home Office Crime Department between 1982 and 1990, they were 'successful in the visible reduction of known juvenile offending' (cited in Goldson, 1997b, p.79). Indeed faith in the effectiveness and rationality of decarceration was such, that penal reform organisations confidently advocated 'phasing out prison department custody for juvenile offenders' and 'replacing custody' (Nacro, 1989a and 1989b), and commentators have since reflected that 'in the early 1990s it was not inconceivable to suppose that the... imprisonment of children might be abolished before the end of the century' (Moore, 2000, p. 116). Government support for this progressive direction in penal policy was always contingent however, and its fortunes ultimately depended upon the extent to which it continued to suit wider political priorities.

Law and policy 1994-present: penal expansion

'The increases in custody rates and sentence length strongly suggest that sentencers have become more severe. This greater severity undoubtedly reflects, in part, a more punitive legislative and legal framework of sentencing. Legislation, guideline judgements and sentence guidelines have all had an inflationery effect on sentences passed. At the same time, the climate of political and media debate about crime and sentencing has become more punitive, and is also likely to have influenced sentencing practice'. (Hough et al, 2003, p. 2)

In the early 1990s, and for a variety of reasons that are explored in greater detail elsewhere (see for example, Davis and Bourhill, 1997; Goldson, 1997a; 2002a and 2004b; Hay, 1995; Haydon and Scraton, 2000; Muncie, 2004), the question of children and crime was dramatically re-politicised and re-profiled in England and Wales. Furthermore, such processes have endured as 'law and order has become a trophy with the political parties jockeying to show who is toughest on crime' (Kennedy, 1995, p.4). Despite the dual effectiveness of diversion and decarceration, first in significantly reducing the levels of child imprisonment and, second, in containing the incidence and gravity of juvenile crime, government ministers and their policy advisors, intent on expressing 'tough' approaches, have turned again to penal custody. Indeed, Garland detects:

'... a new relationship between politicians, the public and penal experts ... in which politicians are more directive, penal experts are less influential, and public opinion becomes a key reference point for evaluating options. Criminal justice is now more vulnerable to shifts of public mood and political reaction ... The populist current in contemporary crime policy is, to some extent, a political posture or tactic, adopted for short term electoral advantage ... Almost inevitably the demand is for more effective penal control ... What this amounts to is a kind of retaliatory law-making, acting out the punitive urges and controlling anxieties of expressive justice. Its chief aims are to assuage popular outrage, reassure the public, and restore 'credibility' of the system, all of which are political rather than penological concerns'. (Garland, 2001, pp. 172-173)

Thus, throughout the 1990s political priorities and 'electoral anxieties' (Pitts, 2000) eclipsed penological rationality, as the punitive urges that apparently characterise modern times imposed greater purchase over the shape and direction of law and policy.

The net effect of successive legislative and policy developments over the last decade or so, has been to completely reverse the decarcerative priorities (both in terms of penal remands and sentences) that characterised legal statutes throughout the 1980s and into the 1990s (up to and including the Criminal Justice Act 1991):

• The Criminal Justice and Public Order Act 1994 ushered in new punitive powers in three particularly significant ways. First, the Act extended the provisions of the Children and Young Persons Act 1933 in respect of children convicted of 'grave crimes'. Section 53 of the Children and Young Persons Act 1933 provided for the detention of children aged 14-17 years for up to the adult maximum, including life, for 'grave' offences carrying maximum sentences of 14 years or more in the case of an adult. The Criminal Justice and Public Order Act 1994 extended these provisions for 10-13 year olds which meant that from January 1995 10-13 year olds convicted at the Crown Court of offences carrying maximum sentences of 14 years or more in the case of an adult, were also exposed to the prospect of being detained for up to the adult maximum. Second, the Criminal Justice Act 1991 set the determinate sentence of detention in a Young Offender Institution ,ɔ-16 year old children) at 12 months. From February 1995 this was doubled to 24 months under the provisions of the Criminal Justice and Public Order Act 1994. Third, and perhaps most significant of all, the 1994 Act introduced a new custodial sentence for 12-14 year old children – the Secure Training Order – to be served in a privately owned and managed children's jail (a Secure Training Centre) for terms up to 24 months. This effectively reversed the decarcerative provisions of youth justice law and policy, in respect of children of such age, that dated back to the Children Act 1908 (Rutherford, 1995).

- The Crime and Disorder Act 1998 introduced a new custodial sentence for 12-17 year old children, the Detention and Training Order. This became operational in April 2000 and it replaced the sentence of Detention in a Young Offender Institution and the Secure Training Order. The term of a Detention and Training Order can be set at 4, 6, 8, 10, 12, 18 or 24 months. It is served half in penal custody and half in the community, although the Act allows for varying the balance of the sentence (including extending the custodial element) depending upon assessments of the child's progress. Children spend the custodial element of the sentence in one of three types of penal setting: a Young Offender Institution; a Secure Training Centre or a Local Authority Secure Children's Home. 'Placement' should be informed by the child's age, gender and perceived level of 'vulnerability' (the convention being that 12-14-year olds, girls and the most vulnerable boys are prioritised for non-Young Offender Institution settings), although in reality the availability of places normally determines the child's custodial destination. The overwhelming majority of places available within the 'Juvenile Secure Estate' are located within the Prison Service's Young Offender Institutions, and detailed research has indicated that many manifestly vulnerable children are thus inappropriately placed in such institutions (Goldson, 2002b). This is a crucial point to which we shall return.

- The Powers of the Criminal Courts (Sentencing) Act 2000 contained provisions (at sections 90-92) for the sentencing of children convicted of 'grave crimes', following the repeal on 25 August 2000 of section 53 of the Children and Young Persons Act 1933. According to Bateman (2002), when combined with the Detention and Training Order provisions of the Crime and Disorder Act 1998, sections 90-92 of the 2000 Act comprise a 'recipe for injustice'.

- The Criminal Justice and Police Act 2001 (at section 130) served to significantly relax the remand criteria in respect of children. The Act empowered the courts to remand children to locked institutions in cases

where they had 'repeatedly' committed offences whilst on bail (including shoplifting, petty theft and criminal damage), irrespective of whether or not such offences were adjudged to expose the public to 'serious harm'. The term 'repeatedly' has been defined in case law as meaning 'on more than one occasion' (Monaghan *et al*, 2003, p. 31). Thus, section 130 of the Criminal Justice and Police Act 2001 effectively replaced the long-established 'seriousness' threshold with a 'nuisance' test. The estimated impact of the legislation was initially thought to be so significant that it was widely believed that implementation would be stalled until additional capacity was provided within the 'Juvenile Secure Estate'. However, in an unexpected announcement in April 2002, the Home Secretary stated that the new powers were to be implemented with immediate effect in ten 'pilot' areas. Moreover, the Criminal Justice and Police Act 2001 (Commencement No. 6) Order 2002 specified that the section 130 provisions would be implemented in all remaining areas of England and Wales in September 2002. In the four months immediately following implementation of the pilot phase, the child remand population in Secure Training Centres and Local Authority Secure Children's Homes increased by 20 per cent (Monaghan *et al*, 2003, p. 31). By imposing additional demands upon Secure Training Centres and Local Authority Secure Children's Homes in this way, the legislation inevitably meant that the already limited capacity of the 'Juvenile Secure Estate' to accommodate the most vulnerable 15- and 16-year old children in non-Prison Service institutions was significantly further curtailed (Goldson, 2002b, pp. 72-74).
• The Criminal Justice Act 2003 provided courts with new custodial powers in respect of children regarded as 'dangerous', allowing longer periods of detention. Such powers are predicated upon actuarial imperatives and are designed for use in cases where 'risk' is predicted, as distinct from comprising proportionate responses to offences actually committed. These powers will almost certainly produce longer custodial sentences for identifiable children and young people (Nacro, 2004a).

Overall, therefore, the cumulative effect of the above – and related developments in law and policy – was to substantially expand the practice of detaining children in penal custody. The expansionist drive, however, bears virtually no relation to either the incidence or the seriousness of youth crime.

Children and crime: contemporary statistical trends

Overall crime has fallen by five per cent according to the BCS [British Crime Survey]... Since the 1995 BCS, crime has fallen by 39 per cent, with vehicle crime and burglary falling by roughly half and violent crime falling by over a third during this period. The risk of becoming a victim of crime has fallen from 40 per cent in 1995 to 26 per cent according to BCS interviews in 2003/04, the lowest level recorded since the BCS began in 1981'. (Dodd *et al*, 2004, p. 7).

The related claims that the expanding penal population in England and Wales is symptomatic of increasing volume and seriousness of crime and/or it represents the only means of preventing crime, are not uncommon. Both claims are fallacious, however, as the government's Prisons Minister (rather ironically) explained in 2004:

'The increase in severity of sentencing bears no relation whatsoever to an increase in criminality or seriousness of offending; it is simply an increase in the seriousness of penalties that are meted out, and we have to tackle that because there is no evidence that it is reducing reoffending rates'. (Paul Goggins, cited in House of Lords House of Commons Joint Committee on Human Rights, 2004b, para. 121)

The Minister's observations are well grounded and are supported by a wealth of authoritative evidence (see, for example, Hough *et al*, 2003; Coulsfield, 2004). The spectacular failure of penal custody in preventing youth crime is examined later in the chapter. First, however, it is important to consider youth crime itself.

Contrary to widely held perceptions, children are *not* responsible for the majority of recorded and detected crimes. In 2001 for example, almost 88 per cent of detected crime in England was committed by adults (Nacro, 2003). More significantly, statistics reveal that the incidence of youth crime appears in decline. Home Office data suggests that between 1992 and 2001 the number of 10-17 year olds cautioned or convicted of indictable offences fell by 21 per cent from 143,600 to 113,800 (Home Office, 2002). Such decline is not simply attributable to demographic change (that is, fewer children in the overall population), as it is also expressed in proportionate terms. The number of children per 100,000 of the population cautioned, reprimanded, warned or convicted of an indictable offence fell from 2,673 in 1992 to 1,927 in 2001 (*ibid.*).

Just as the incidence of youth crime tends to be 'amplified' within the realm of public perception (and in many cases 'official' representation), so too does its gravity and seriousness. The typical perception of violent offences against the person is misleading. Most offences committed by children are directed against property. The categories of offences generally regarded as the least serious, that is theft and handling stolen goods, comprised almost half of recorded crime attributable to children in 2001 (Home Office, 2002). In actual fact, violent offences against the person account for less than 14 per cent, and robbery – primarily 'taking mobile telephones' (Harrington and Mayhew, 2001) – for only 2.4 per cent, of all offences for which children were held to be responsible (for a fuller discussion see Goldson, 2004b).

Children convicted for criminal offences are predominantly male. Boys consistently account for almost 80 per cent of detected youth crime, and the available data does not bear out the common perception that girls are more inclined to offend now, than they were previously (Worrall, 1999; Nacro, 2004b). Boys also tend to commit the more serious offences. Regarding ethnicity, black children and young people are no more likely than their white counterparts to commit offences (Graham and Bowling, 1995; Home Office, 2004a; Webster, forthcoming, 2006). Bearing these points in mind, the disproportionate increase in the penal detention of girls over boys, and the manifest over-representation of black children in penal custody, is anomalous. Indeed, such phenomena are more indicative of the intrinsic gendered and racialised injustices of the youth 'justice' process, than they are of the offending proclivities of any identifiable group of children.

Whilst it is always necessary to exercise care and caution in reading, analysing and interpreting 'official' youth crime data (Muncie, 2004, pp. 15-19), the contradiction between the stable, if not diminishing, patterns of youth crime on the one hand, and law and policy allowing for substantial penal expansion on the other, is striking.

Children in penal custody: contemporary statistical trends

'... [T]he Committee notes with serious concern that the situation of children in conflict with the law has worsened since the consideration of the initial report [in 1995]... The Committee is particularly concerned that... children between 12 and 14 years of age are now being deprived of their liberty. More generally, the Committee is deeply concerned at the high increasing numbers of children in custody, at earlier ages for lesser offences, and for longer custodial sentences imposed by the recent increased court powers to give detention and training orders. Therefore, it is the concern of the Committee that deprivation of liberty is not being used only as a measure of last resort and for the shortest appropriate period of time, in violation of article 37(b) of the Convention'. (United Nations Committee on the Rights of the Child, 2002, para. 57)

'We urge the Government to re-examine, with renewed urgency... policy
and practice... with the specific aim of reducing the number of young
people entering custody'. (House of Lords House of Commons Joint
Committee on Human Rights, 2003, para. 41)

Total rates of imprisonment in England and Wales have escalated
significantly in recent times. In 1994 the average prison population was 48,631
but by 1997 it had risen to 60,131 (Prison Reform Trust, 2004a, p. 3). This
pattern of penal expansion has continued since the first New Labour
administration took office in 1997. In 2002, for example, the *average* prison
population, at 70,860, was higher than in any previous year (Councell, 2003,
p. 1; Home Office 2003a, p. 3). By March 2004 however, the *total* prison
population exceeded 75,000 (Howard League for Penal Reform, 2004a) and,
by May 2005, it had reached more than 76,000 for the first time in penal
history (British Broadcasting Corporation, 2005). Expressed as a rate per
100,000 of the national population, the prison population in England and
Wales is now the highest among countries of the European Union (Home
Office, 2003b). It is no surprise, therefore, that prison overcrowding is
endemic and some prisons exceed their maximum capacity (that is the 'safe'
overcrowded capacity) (Her Majesty's Chief Inspector of Prisons, 2005; Prison
Reform Trust, 2004a).

Contemporary statistical trends in relation to children in penal custody
follow similar contours. The total number of custodial sentences imposed upon
children rose from approximately 4,000 per annum in 1992 to 7,600 in 2001, a
90 per cent increase (Nacro, 2003 and 2005). During the same period the child
remand population grew by 142 per cent (Goldson, 2002b). In March 2004,
there were 3,251 children and young people (10-18 years) in penal custody in
England and Wales: 2,772 in Prison ServiceYoung Offender Institutions; 290 in
Local Authority Secure Children's Homes and 189 in privately managed Secure
Training Centres (Youth Justice Board, 2005, p.78). Furthermore, within this
general trend of penal expansion seven 'sub-trends' are discernible.

Children in penal custody – comparative European rates

Table 1 shows the number of children detained in penal custody in ten
European jurisdictions/countries.

Comparative analyses of youth justice systems in general, and rates of child
imprisonment in particular, are extraordinarily difficult (Muncie, 2003 and
2005; Muncie and Goldson, forthcoming, 2006). Truly comparable statistical
data is not readily available and what counts as 'custody' varies between

Table 1:	Children in Penal Custody in Selected European Countries		
Jurisdiction/ Country	Number of Children in Penal Custody (Date)	Number of Children in Population – Millions	Rate in Penal Custody per 1,000 of Child Population
Finland	2 (23.10.02)	1.131	0.002
Sweden	12 (01.10.98)	1.914	0.006
Denmark	9 (01.09.00)	1.134	0.008
Spain	152 (31.12.00)	7.341	0.02
Netherlands	120 (01.09.00)	3.455	0.034
Belgium	96 (01.09.00)	2.137	0.05
France	862 (01.05.02)	13.456	0.06
Portugal	214 (31.12.99)	2.052	0.1
Austria	201 (01.09.98)	1.634	0.12
England and Wales	3,133 (30.09.02)	13.351	0.23

Source: Nacro (2003, p. 9)

jurisdictions. Certain care is required in interpreting the data that is available, therefore. For example, it is important to note that the figures represented in Table 1 relate to different periods of time. Notwithstanding this, four points are particularly noteworthy:

• First, the figures expose very significant cross-jurisdictional variations and England and Wales is the jurisdiction substantially most inclined to hold children in penal custody.
• Second, of the ten jurisdictions listed perhaps France is the best single comparator to England and Wales given its similar, although slightly higher, number of children in the overall population (at just under 13.5 million). However, in England and Wales almost four times as many children are detained in penal custody.
• Third, Finland is the country that is least inclined to hold children in penal custody. If the number of children in Finland is multiplied by 12 it gives a figure of 13.572 millions, which is comparable to the total number of children in England and Wales. However, if the number of children detained

in penal custody in Finland is similarly multiplied by 12 it gives a figure of 24. In other words, if children in England and Wales were detained at the same rate as their Finnish counterparts 24 would be in penal custody as opposed to 3,133. In proportionate terms, therefore, children are 130 times more likely to be detained in penal custody in England and Wales than they are in Finland.

• Fourth, if the child populations of Finland, Sweden, Denmark, Spain, the Netherlands Belgium, France, Portugal and Austria are combined it gives a total of 34.254 million children. Within this combined population 1,668 children are held in penal custody. Thus almost twice as many children are detained in England and Wales (with a population of 13.351 million children) as there are in the other nine jurisdictions combined (with a population of 34.254 million children). England and Wales, therefore, is a peculiarly punitive jurisdiction for children.

Length of sentence

In addition to substantial increases in the numbers of children being held in penal custody in England and Wales over the last decade, sentences have also increased in length over the same period as can be seen from Tables 2 and 3. The average length of custodial sentence for 15-17 year old boys rose from 9.2 months in 1992 to 12.2 months in 2002, and for girls of the same age the corresponding figures stood at 8.1 and 11.4 months.

Long term detention

The figures above exclude sentences of long-term detention. Since 1994, however, the number of children sentenced in this way has also risen considerably. Graham and Moore (2004, p.20) note that:

'In 1970 only six [long term] sentences were imposed... By the early 1990s this had risen to about 100 juveniles, but by 1997 more than 700 were [so] sentenced. This is partly due to the widening of the range of crimes covered... and the lowering of the eligibility threshold to 10, but even taking this into account there has clearly been a real increase in the use of these sentencing powers. It is perhaps not surprising that the UK (including Scotland and Northern Ireland) have one of the highest rates of custody in Europe and this fuels the concern that the detention of juveniles in England and Wales is neither used as a measure of last resort nor for the shortest possible period of time'.

Table 2:	Average sentence length in months of boys (aged 15-17 years) in penal custody 1992-2002 (excluding those sentenced to life)		
Year	Crown Court	Magistrates Court	All courts
1992	14.8	4.6	9.2
1993	16.4	5.1	8.6
1994	16.5	5.2	8.5
1995	17.3	5.2	9.6
1996	20.0	5.5	11.1
1997	20.5	5.4	11.6
1998	19.4	5.1	10.7
1999	18.7	4.7	10.3
2000	19.6	6.4	10.5
2001	20.3	7.2	10.4
2002	22.0	8.1	12.2

Source: Home Office, 2003a, p. 78.

Table 3:	Average sentence length in months of girls (aged 15-17 years) in penal custody 1992-2002 (excluding those sentenced to life)		
Year	Crown Court	Magistrates Court	All courts
1992	11.4	4.2	8.1
1993	13.3	3.7	6.9
1994	14.8	4.1	8.2
1995	18.5	3.5	10.0
1996	15.1	4.3	8.3
1997	15.6	3.7	9.6
1998	14.1	3.9	7.6
1999	14.3	3.6	7.1
2000	15.8	5.5	8.6
2001	19.4	5.8	9.4
2002	20.0	7.0	11.4

Source: Home Office, 2003a, p. 78.

The age of child prisoners

As we have discussed, legislative reforms – most notably the Criminal Justice and Public Order Act 1994 and the Crime and Disorder Act 1998 – have provided for the detention of younger children. Nacro (2003, p. 12) has observed: 'as a result the detention of children under the age of 15 years has become routine'. In 1992 approximately 100 such children were sentenced to custody, in 2001 however, 800 children aged 12-14 years were similarly sentenced, an increase of 800 per cent (Home Office, 2002). As indicated earlier, the provisions allowing for the 'routine' penal detention of 12-14-year-old children have reversed a policy direction in England and Wales that dated back to the Children Act 1908 (Rutherford, 1995). Many penal reform and criminal justice authorities expressed substantial opposition to such measures as they made their passage through the parliamentary process (see for example, Penal Affairs Consortium, 1994). The determination of the Conservative Government to push the legislation through remained intact, however. The Parliamentary Opposition showed less resolve. Although New Labour opposed various aspects of the Criminal Justice and Public Order Bill in its committee stages, it abstained during the final vote (Howard League, 1995, p.3), effectively acceding to the increase in the number of child prisoners and the introduction of privately managed jails for 12 to 14 year-olds.

The gendered distribution of penal custody

More girls are being locked up than previously and the rate of growth is proportionately higher than that for boys. Although the baseline comprises relatively small numbers, the use of penal custody in relation to girls since 1993 has increased by 500 per cent (Nacro, 2003, p. 12). Furthermore, girls are regularly detained alongside adult prisoners, a practice that has been seriously questioned by child welfare agencies, penal reform organisations and Her Majesty's Chief Inspector of Prisons alike. Following a case taken to the High Court by the Howard League for Penal Reform the Judge, Mr Justice Hooper, commented: 'it is difficult to see how it can be said to be in the best interests of a 16 year old, such as the claimant, to spend a considerable amount of time on association with those 18 and over' (cited in Howard League for Penal Reform, 2004, p. 1). Furthermore, following a prison inspection Her Majesty's Chief Inspector of Prisons explained:

'At our last inspection, we expressed serious concern about conditions and treatment of... girls held there... Since that inspection, the prison's population has become if anything more difficult to manage... The number of girls... has also increased, in spite of repeated assurances that under-18s would no longer be held in Prison Service custody'. (Her Majesty's Chief Inspector of Prisons, 2004a, p. 3)

Racism and the racialisation of penal custody

Despite the statutory duty that applies to all 'persons engaged in the administration of criminal justice' to 'avoid discriminating against any persons on the grounds of race' (section 95(1)(b) Criminal Justice Act 1991), racism is endemic throughout the youth justice system and the substantial over-representation of black children continues to prevail at every discrete stage from pre-arrest to post-sentence (Goldson and Chigwada-Bailey, 1999). This 'corrosive disease' (Macpherson, 1999, para 6.34) means that black children are: more likely (than their white counterparts) to be remanded and/or sentenced to penal custody; more likely to be detained for disproportionately long terms; and more likely to encounter additional adversity (whilst detained) derived from racist encounters (Cowan, 2005). Indeed, Ashton and Grindrod (1999, p. 177) have reflected on the 'hugely disproportionate use of prison custody being made in respect of black children' and similar findings have been reported by many others (see for example, Bowling and Phillips, 2002). More recent research has revealed that young black males are 6.7 times more likely than white boys to have custodial sentences in excess of 12 months imposed upon them in the Crown Court (Feilzer and Hood, 2004). Following his detailed interviews with young black prisoners Wilson (2004, p. 328) reports that 'time and again... extreme forms of racism were described'. Indeed, the Director General of the Prison Service has acknowledged that the prison system is 'institutionally racist' (cited in Goldson, 2001a, p. 19) and Her Majesty's Chief Inspector of Prisons has commented:

'I have long been concerned that the biggest single problem facing the Director General is the culture that still pervades parts of the prison system ... It is a culture that adopts an attitude to prisoners that is not only judgmental, but too often includes physical and mental brutality... One of its most obvious manifestations is in attitudes to minorities, of whatever kind, who are treated not as equal but as unequal because of their minority status. There are ... minority groups whose inequality of treatment concerns me – ethnic or cultural minorities'. (Her Majesty's Chief Inspector of Prisons, 2001, p. 16)

No relief

The most recent statistics pertaining to children in penal custody are particularly worrying. Following what appears to have been a temporary and short-lived dip in the number of child prisoners (Youth Justice Board for England and Wales, 2003), the Chairperson of the Youth Justice Board for England and Wales has reported that the first four months of 2004 were marked by a further 10 per cent increase (Morgan, 2004). This is located within a wider context in which Home Office statisticians predict that given current expansionist trends the total prison population is set to reach between 98,900 and 109,600 by June 2009 (Councell and Simes, 2002). Inevitably such patterns of continued expansion will intensify pressures on a system that is already failing to meet the needs of vulnerable child prisoners (Goldson, 2002b). Overcrowding means that prisons become 'less safe', 'less constructive' and 'harder to run' (Howard League for Penal Reform, 2004a, pp. 3-4) and, as a consequence, they become less attentive to the duty of care required for all prisoners, especially for the most vulnerable child prisoners.

Child prisoners

'The picture for young prisoners... is extreme... These statistics describe a group of young people ... isolated, victimised and disturbed. Many of them have experienced significant trauma and disruption in their domestic lives and their schooling, and are without the personal and social support they need to overcome their difficulties and begin to manage their lives and relationships. Many are mentally, emotionally and morally immature... Before any work can be done to sensitise them to the needs of others and the impact of their offending on victims, their own needs as maturing adolescents for care, support and direction have to be met'. (Her Majesty's Chief Inspector of Prisons, 2000, p. 25)

'... I am a child. They should understand that when they're sending us all to prison'. (Cited in Lyon, Dennison and Wilson, 2000, p.32)

Child prisoners are routinely drawn from some of the most disadvantaged families, neighbourhoods and communities in England and Wales. Children for whom the fabric of life invariably stretches across poverty; family discord; public care; drug and alcohol misuse; mental distress; ill-health; emotional, physical and sexual abuse; self-harm; homelessness; isolation; loneliness; circumscribed educational and employment opportunities; and the most pressing sense of distress and alienation, are the very children routinely held in penal custody. Indeed, as Her Majesty's Chief Inspector of Prisons (1999a, p.3) observed, penal detention often marks 'just one further stage in the exclusion of a group of children who between them, have already experienced almost every form of social exclusion on offer'.

Family circumstances

An in-depth study of children held in penal custody whilst on remand found that 48 per cent were living apart from any member of their family immediately prior to entering prison, including 12 per cent who were being 'looked after' by the Local Authority and a further 12 per cent who literally had nowhere to live and were having to survive on the street. Whilst most of the children identified the need for adult support and advice, 68 per cent reported that throughout their experience of 'growing up' there was no-one to whom they could turn for such guidance (Goldson, 2002b, pp.130-131). The findings from this relatively small-scale study are consistent with those drawn from wider ranging surveys. Thus approximately half of children held in penal custody have been, or remain, involved with Social Services Departments and a significant proportion have biographies scarred by adult abuse and violation (see, for example: Children's Rights Alliance for England, 2002; Social Exclusion Unit, 2002a; Social Services Inspectorate *et al*, 2002; The Association of Directors of Social Services *et al*, 2003; Prison Reform Trust, 2004a; Challen and Walton, 2004; Holmes and Gibbs, 2004).

Education

In a major review of the educational needs of children in penal custody, Her Majesty's Chief Inspector of Prisons and the Office for Standards in Education (2001, p.10) found that: 84 per cent of child prisoners had been excluded from school; 86 per cent had regularly not attended school; 52 per cent had left school aged 14 years or younger; 29 per cent had left school aged 13 years or younger and 73 per cent described their educational achievement as 'nil'. It is of no surprise, therefore, that over 25 per cent of child prisoners have literacy and numeracy skills equivalent to a 7-year-old (Social Exclusion Unit, 2002a) and 'most' have 'very significant learning needs and problems' (Social Services Inspectorate *et al*, 2002, p. 70).

Health

In a thematic review of 'young prisoners' Her Majesty's Chief Inspector of Prisons (1997, p. 45) concluded that 'a very significant proportion of the population of young people in custody need help with health care'. Similarly, the British Medical Association (2001, pp. 1 and 5), commenting upon the relationship between poverty, disadvantage and poor health, observed:

'... patients within prison are amongst the most needy in the country in relation to their health care needs. Over 90 per cent of patients who reside in our jails come from deprived backgrounds... 17 per cent of young offenders were not registered with a general practitioner and generally the young people had a low level of contact with primary health care'.

Furthermore, Her Majesty's Chief Inspector of Prisons (1997, p.45) also reported that 'over 50 per cent of young prisoners on remand and 30 per cent of sentenced young offenders have a diagnosable mental disorder'. Lader et al (2000), in their wide-ranging study of 'psychiatric morbidity' among children and young people in prison found that: 84 per cent of remand prisoners had a 'personality disorder'; 8 per cent had a psychotic disorder; 60 per cent had sleep problems; 70 per cent had 'hazardous drinking' habits; 93 per cent reported using drugs prior to remand and 'male young offenders on remand were the most likely to report having suffered ... stressful life events'. (see also, Social Exclusion Unit, 2002a). Moreover, and not surprisingly, the experience of imprisonment itself has been identified as having a deleterious effect on the physical and mental well-being of children (Her Majesty's Chief Inspector of Prisons 1997; Farrant, 2001; Leech and Cheney, 2001; Mental Health Foundation, 1999).

In sum, when taking account of the backgrounds and personal circumstances of child prisoners 'it is evident that on any count this is a significantly deprived, excluded, and abused population of children, who are in serious need of a variety of services' (Association of Directors of Social Services et al, 2003, p. 6) and the 'Juvenile Secure Estate' is 'not equipped to meet their needs' (Her Majesty's Chief Inspector of Prisons, 2000, pp. 69-70).

Conditions and treatment

'Young prisoners often need more of everything. They need more one to one attention, more supervision, more contact with staff, more contact with each other, more protection from themselves and other people, more challenging, more reassurance, more understanding and more forgiveness'. (Her Majesty's Chief Inspector of Prisons, 1997, p. 63)

'In recent years the massively increased numbers of children sent to custody have been dumped on prison service establishments, in a prison system that has not, traditionally, recognised that it has a role in caring for children in need of care, development and control. Within this system children are, quite frankly, lost'. (Her Majesty's Chief Inspector of Prisons, 1997, p. 63)

The 'Juvenile Secure Estate' comprises three different types of institution each managed within a different 'penal domain':

• 24 Local Authority Secure Children's Homes (LASCHs) that are managed by Social Services Departments under the national aegis of the Department for Education and Skills (Secure Accommodation Network, 2005). LASCHs are generally regarded as being the most 'child-centred' institutions within the 'juvenile secure estate' and, in addition to providing 'justice' placements for children on penal remand and/or serving custodial sentences, the LASCHs are also licensed to provide 'welfare' placements for children whose liberty is restricted via civil proceedings in the Family Proceedings Courts (for a fuller discussion see Goldson, 2002b). In October 2004 there were 235 'justice' places available in LASCHs (Youth Justice Board, 2004a, p.12). This represents a diminishing stock, not least because the Youth Justice Board for England and Wales decided to reduce significantly the number of placements it commissioned in LASCHs in 2004-05. Since 2004, six LASCHs have closed (Secure Accommodation Network, 2005).
• 4 Secure Training Centres (STCs) that are provided by the private sector. Rebound ECD, a subsidiary of Group 4, manages Medway and Rainsbrook STCs and Premier Training Services Limited runs Hassockfield and Oakhill STCs. Rebound ECD and Premier Training Services Limited have each contracted with the Home Office/Youth Justice Board for England and Wales to provide placements. In October 2004 there were 274 places available in STCs (Youth Justice Board, 2004a, p.12);
• 17 Young Offender Institutions (YOIs) which are the responsibility of the Prison Service. In October 2004 there were 2,700 places available in YOIs for children aged 15-17 years (Youth Justice Board, 2004a, p.12).

Local Authority Secure Children's Homes and, to a lesser extent Secure Training Centres, are relatively small when compared with Young Offender Institutions. Thus, the overwhelming majority of children in penal custody are held in the 17 Prison Service establishments. Moreover, the size of penal institutions is particularly important in respect of conditions and treatment:

'One of the most important factors in creating a safe environment is size. The other places where children are held – Secure Units and Secure Training Centres – are small, with a high staff-child ratio. The Prison Service, however, may hold children in what we regard as unacceptably high numbers and units. Units of 60 disturbed and damaged adolescent boys are unlikely to be safe... There are therefore already significant barriers to the Prison Service being able to provide a safe and positive environment for children; and the question whether it should continue to do so is a live one. Yet during the year the number of children has risen, to close to 3,000, and looks set to rise further. Promises to reduce unit size... are further than ever from being delivered'. (Her Majesty's Chief Inspector of Prisons, 2002a, pp. 36-37. See also: Goldson, 2002b, pp. 64-66; Holmes and Gibbs, 2004, p. 7)

Thus the juxtaposition of the opening statements from Her Majesty's Chief Inspector of Prisons above (taken from a major thematic review of children and young people in penal custody) is telling. The vulnerabilities and needs of children in penal custody are well-established, but the prison system is essentially ill-equipped to meet them.

In recent years, the Youth Justice Board for England and Wales and the Prison Service have together implemented a programme of 'substantial reform' (Her Majesty's Chief Inspector of Prisons, 2002a, p. 34) designed to improve the conditions and treatment of children in penal custody. It is important to recognise that despite such reforms, the best efforts of some members of staff and signs of 'considerable improvement' (Her Majesty's Chief Inspector of Prisons, 2004b, p. 44) in some Young Offender Institutions, 'the ability [of prisons] even to provide a safe and decent environment for a growing and increasingly damaged and demanding population' (Her Majesty's Chief Inspector of Prisons, 2004b, p. 4) remains profoundly deficient.

The Children's Rights Alliance for England (2002) undertook a detailed analysis of the conditions and treatment experienced by children in penal custody, drawing on reports prepared by Her Majesty's Inspectorate of Prisons. The results were illuminating: widespread neglect in relation to physical and mental health; endemic bullying, humiliation and ill-treatment (staff-on-child and child-on-child); racism and other forms of discrimination; systemic invasion of privacy; long and uninterrupted periods of cell-based confinement; deprivation of fresh air and exercise; inadequate educational and rehabilitative provision; insufficient opportunities to maintain contact with family; poor diet;

ill-fitting clothing in poor state of repair; a shabby physical environment; and, in reality, virtually no opportunity to complain and/or make representations. All of these negative and neglectful processes define the conditions within which children are routinely held in penal custody (*ibid*, pp. 49-137). Even if the reform efforts mentioned above were 'very much welcomed' by Her Majesty's Chief Inspector of Prisons in 2002 (Her Majesty's Chief Inspector of Prisons, 2002a, p. 34), by 2004 the same Chief Inspector continued to express 'serious concerns about the safety of children' (Her Majesty's Chief Inspector of Prisons, 2004, p. 44). Furthermore, in 2002 the moribund conditions and treatment to which many children are exposed in penal custody led Mr Justice Munby, a High Court Judge, to conclude that:

> 'They ought to be – I hope they are – matters of the very greatest concern to the Prison Service, to the Secretary of State for the Home Department and, indeed, to society at large. For these are things being done to children by the State – by all of us – in circumstances where the State appears to be failing, and in some instances failing very badly, in its duties to vulnerable and damaged children... [these are] matters which, on the face of it, ought to shock the conscience of every citizen'. (Munby, 2002, paras. 172 and 175)

The human costs of penal custody

> 'Prisons collect [children] who find it difficult to cope, they collect excessive numbers of [children] with mental disorder, they collect [children] who have weak social supports, they collect [children] who, by any objective test, do not have rosy prospects. This collection of [children] is humiliated and stigmatised by the process of arrest, police inquiry and court appearance. [Child] prisoners suffer the ultimate ignominy of banishment to an uncongenial institution, which is often overcrowded, where friends cannot be chosen, and physical conditions are spartan. Above all, they are by the process separated from everything familiar, including all their social supports and loved ones, however unsatisfactory. This is what is supposed to happen, and this is what the punishment of prison is all about'. (Gunn, cited in Her Majesty's Chief Inspector of Prisons, 1999b, p.25)

Penal custody for children cannot be a neutral experience. Separation from familiar conditions itself – family, friends, home and community – however unsatisfactory the conditions might be, has a deleterious effect. When the child is separated from the familiar by removal to the uncongenial environment of penal custody, the sense of loss is compounded. Indeed, the consequences of placing damaged children in damaging environments are predictable: family relations invariably become more strained; negative behavioural traits are normally reinforced; experience of bullying, intimidation and violence in myriad forms is widespread; alienation is compounded; institutionalisation is a risk and stigmatisation is a certainty.

Bullying, in all of its forms, is a particular problem that exerts substantial human costs on children in penal custody, especially Young Offender Institutions. Perhaps the most obvious expression of bullying is physical assault, much of which goes unreported – thus unrecorded – owing to the intense antipathy to the practice of 'grassing' within prison culture, and worse still the consequences of being labelled a 'grass'. In one Young Offender Institution between 2000 and 2001, 222 assaults were recorded in a twelve month period giving an assault rate of 93 per cent (the rate of assault is measured by the number of proven adjudications of assault as a percentage of the average prisoner population) (Howard League for Penal Reform, 2001a, p. 8). More recently, 56 per cent of children surveyed by Her Majesty's Chief Inspector of Prisons (2005, p. 56) in one Young Offender Institution reported that they had felt 'unsafe', 'nearly a quarter said they had been hit, kicked or assaulted' and there 'had been 150 proven assaults in eight months'. Physical assault, or physical abuse, is clearly commonplace in penal custody and black children are particulary victimised (Cowan, 2005). Furthermore, children are also exposed to other forms of 'bullying' including sexual assault; verbal abuse (including name-calling; threats; racist, sexist and homophobic taunting); extortion and theft; and lending and trading cultures – particularly in relation to tobacco – involving exorbitant rates of interest that accumulate on a daily basis (Goldson, 2002b).

Bullying is extremely difficult to identify, it may be transmitted by no more than a look-in-the-eye. Furthermore, staff-child ratios are so stretched within penal custody that levels of supervision inevitably are strained. Bullying is insuffiently 'managed' and contagious. It is entrenched within the fabric of prison life. The bullied child may also be a bully, the victim and aggressor 'selves' intersect and overlap, the damaged wreak damage:

> 'This is the self who knows he has always fought for things and caused trouble, who needs love in order to grasp at a feeling of safety which has eluded him all his life, who does bad things to himself and to others because he is a bad and evil person, who has been so troubled by feeling unsafe all his life that he grasps greedily at every bit of power that comes his way. This self has a tender and caring side, but not one that can be

sustained. Threatened with pain, even if only in the form of hurtful remarks, this is a self that lashes out'. (Medlicott, 2001, p. 172)

For all child prisoners, the harsh conditions of penal custody perpetuate misery and fear. For some, especially those in Young Offender Institutions, it is literally too much to bear:

'Last night this kid, I don't know why, I think he was getting bullied but I don't know. One of the Officer's opened this kid's door and he just shouted "get the nurse" and we were all put behind our doors. No-one knew what was going on, but we all knew if you see what I mean. We heard them all rushing around and I reckon we all knew. I knew. I thought about it all night, I couldn't stop thinking about it. This morning when we came out for breakfast the screws said that he had tried to kill himself and he was in hospital on a life support machine. At dinner they said he was dead. He was sixteen, the same age as me. Everyone was very quiet'. (Boy aged 16yrs, cited in Goldson 2002b, p. 152)

The remarkable and paradoxical fact about the corrosive effect of penal custody on children, is that it is recognised comprehensively by government ministers and major state agencies alike. In answer to a Parliamentary question on June 7, 2004, for example, Paul Goggins, Home Office Minister, confirmed that the numbers of *vulnerable* children placed in Young Offender Institutions have followed upward trajectories each year since 2000. The figures given for children officially assessed as 'vulnerable' and yet still 'placed' in Prison Service establishments by the Youth Justice Board for England and Wales were: 432 for 2000-01; 1,875 for 2001-02; 2,903 for 2002-03 and 3,337 for 2003-04 (cited in Bateman, 2004a). At a time when ever-increasing numbers of vulnerable children are being detained in penal custody, the most senior personnel from eight major statutory inspectorates have concluded that 'young people in YOIs still face the gravest risks to their welfare' (Social Services Inspectorate *et al*, 2002, p. 72). Similarly, Her Majesty's Chief Inspector of Prisons (2005, p.57) has observed that 'some young people are not safe... simply because they should not be there'. Within any other setting this would be described as institutional child abuse; there would be calls for resignations and demands for a comprehensive inquiry. The situation with regard to children in penal settings is quite different, however. Official data attesting to their vulnerabilities, together with repeatedly expressed concerns in respect of their welfare – from the most authoritative sources – appear to be disregarded. The social value of child prisoners seemingly counts for little.

The fiscal costs of penal custody

Although estimates vary, an enormous amount of public money is spent on keeping children in penal custody. The figures in Table 4 are taken from five reports from Her Majesty's Chief Inspector of Prisons. They suggest that the average weekly and yearly costs of keeping a single child in prison is £620.00 and £32,264 respectively.

Other sources suggest that the full fiscal costs of child imprisonment are significantly higher. In 2001 the Youth Justice Board for England and Wales (Dalrymple, 2001, p. 21) calculated that the average daily cost of keeping a single child in a Young Offender Institution was £104.00 (that is £728.00 per week or £37,856 per year). More recently, the Audit Commission (2004, p. 2) reported that 'a six month stay in a young offender institution costs £25,400' (£140.00 per day, £977.00 per week or £50,800 per year). The fiscal costs of

Table 4:	Illustrative fiscal costs of child imprisonment				
Young Offender Institution	**Number of Child Prisoners Held[1]**	**Weekly cost per prisoner £**	**Yearly cost per prisoner £**	**Weekly cost at total number of prisoners £**	**Yearly cost at total number of prisoners £**
Castington[2]	292	570	29,634	166,406	8,653,128
Feltham A[3]	220	777	40,383	170,851	8,884,260
Huntercombe[4]	360	557	28,980	200,615	10,432,800
Onley[5]	541	474	24,668	256,642	13,345,388
Werrington[6]	120	724	37,655	86,896	4,518,600
AVERAGES	-	620	32,264	–	–

Sources: Her Majesty's Chief Inspector of Prisons, 2002b; 2002c; 2003a; 2003b; 2003c.

1. These figures relate to the number of prisoners held at the time of inspection. In addition to child ('juvenile') prisoners aged 15-17 years some of the YOIs also detain 'young adult' prisoners aged 18-21 years (see YOI specific notes below).
2. Castington holds sentenced and remanded juvenile and young adult prisoners.
3. Feltham A holds sentenced and remanded juvenile prisoners only.
4. Huntercombe holds sentenced and remanded juvenile prisoners only
5. Onley holds sentenced and remanded juvenile and sentenced young adult prisoners.
6. Werrington holds sentenced juvenile prisoners only.

holding children in Local Authority Secure Children's Homes and the privately owned and managed Secure Training Centres are substantially more expensive. In 2000 Nathan (2000, p. 6) reported that the average annual costs of holding a single child in a Secure Training Centre ranged from £118,161 to £149,445 (that is £326.00 to £411.00 per day or £2,272 to £2,874 per week). This is consistent with the Youth Justice Board for England and Wales average annual figure of £134,680 (that is £370.00 per day or £2,590 per week) (Dalrymple, 2001, p. 21). The total costs of keeping children in penal custody are extremely high, therefore, and the Chairperson of the Youth Justice Board for England and Wales has reported that £293.5 million was spent for this purpose in 2003-04 alone (Morgan, 2004. See also, House of Commons Committee of Public Accounts, 2004).

These figures tell only part of the fiscal story. They do not include the considerable public expense incurred in processing children through the courts and imposing periods of penal remand and/or custodial sentences. The Social Exclusion Unit (2002, p.2) observed that 'the average cost of a prison sentence imposed at a crown court is roughly £30,500, made up of court and other legal costs'. When the total annual costs of locating children in penal custody are calculated, the £293 million plus of public money spent by the Youth Justice Board for England and Wales, pays only part of the bill.

Bearing in mind what is known about the conditions and treatment to which children are routinely exposed in penal custody, serious questions have to be asked in terms of value for (public) money. Stern (1998, xxi) raised pertinent questions in the 1990s: 'How much imprisonment can a society afford? What shall we have to go without in order to have such a large percentage of people made dependent on state funding?'. Yet there are those who might argue that despite the telling human costs and the substantial financial expense of child imprisonment, it is a price worth paying in order to 'stem the tide' of youth crime. The evidence lends no support for this view.

Penal outcomes

'Section 37 (1) of the Crime and Disorder Act establishes that the principal aim of the youth justice system is "to prevent offending by children and young persons"'. (Her Majesty's Prison Service, 2003, para. 1.3)

'The hard truth is that... juvenile penal institutions have minimal impact on crime. If most prisons were closed tomorrow, the rise in crime would be negligible... incapacitation as the major tenet of crime control is a questionable social policy'. (Miller, 1991, pp.181-182)

Reconviction rates for children discharged from penal custody have always been high. Hagell and Hazel (2001) note that concern with 'poor perfomance' (in terms of reducing re-offending) has been a recurrent theme throughout the history of detaining children in penal custody (see also Goldson, 2004a). Such concern has not faltered in recent years: 'prison sentences are not succeeding in turning the majority of offenders away from crime' (Social Exclusion Unit, 2002, p. 1).

The failure of penal custody to prevent children from re-offending is well illustrated by analysis of reconviction rates that relate to 'the proportion of prisoners discharged from prison [who] are convicted on a further occasion within a given period (usually two years)' (Home Office, 2003a, p. 150). As with the fiscal costs of penal custody, the data on reconviction rates vary. The constant, however, is that the reconviction of children following release from all forms of penal custody is exceptionally high. Moreover, whilst comparative analysis over time is extraordinarily complex, one reading of the evidence suggests that re-conviction rates have heightened in recent years: 'the reconviction rate for males has risen by 8 percentage points since its lowest level in 1992 [and] the reconviction rate for females has increased by 17 percentage points' (Home Office, 2003a, p. 153). Accordingly, in October 2004, a Parliamentary Select Committee reported that re-conviction rates stand at 80 per cent with regard to released child prisoners (House of Commons Committee of Public Accounts, 2004). Despite substantial investment in new sentences, regimes and institutions, therefore, penal custody continues to fail in terms of preventing youth offending.

The Detention and Training Order is the latest custodial sentence relating to children aged 12-17 years. As discussed above, the sentence is provided by the Crime and Disorder Act 1998 and it was first implemented in April 2000. It is served half in penal custody and half in the community. Whilst an evaluation of nearly 6,000 children subject to a Detention and Training Order identified elements of 'good practice', it also reported high rates of re-offending, particularly in the first few weeks following release (Hazel *et al*, 2002). Similarly, recent experiments relating to 'intensive' custodial regimes do not appear to yield positive lasting results in respect of children: 'preliminary findings' suggest that initial 'improvements' in reconviction patterns are unlikely to endure over time (Farrington, *et al*, 2000). Furthermore, the results of research into the more expensive forms of penal custody provide no relief. Despite weekly costs in excess of £2,500 per child, 11 per cent of children discharged from the first of the privately owned and managed Secure Training Centres were arrested for a further offence within 7 days, 52 per cent were similarly arrested within seven weeks and 67 per cent had been arrested within 20 weeks of release (Hagell *et al*, 2000).

There is little, if any, rational justification for the policies and practices of penal expansion. Detaining increasing numbers of children in penal custody intensifies the danger, damage and harm that they face; imposes a substantial burden on the Treasury; and ultimately fails to provide a safer society. There is a pressing need for a comprehensive review of such policies and practices.

Chapter 3
Child Deaths in Penal Custody

'[Children] in custody are peculiarly vulnerable and dependent... I shall take those arguments more or less for granted. I shall simply assert that... because they are in the hands of the state, because the state exercises complete control over them, it follows that the state should take responsibility for them and owes a correlative duty for their care'. (Morgan, 1996, p. 23)

'The death of children fills us all with a particular horror – their life cut short, their potential unfulfilled. But the self-inflicted deaths of children carry two further horrors. First, that the children must have been intolerably unhappy and second, that responsible adults have failed in their primary duty – to keep children safe from harm. In many cases outside prison child suicides come as a surprise, but so far as young offender institutions are concerned this manifestly cannot be the case since *every* child prisoner is known to be at risk of suicide'. (Children's Rights Alliance for England, 2002, pp. 64-5, original emphasis)

'It's getting worser and worser. A kid has just killed himself and I reckon that was through bullying. A sixteen year old lad, a sixteen year old does not kill themself when they have their whole life in front of them. I just picture it in my head and it's bad, it's really bad'. (Child prisoner aged 15, cited in Goldson, 2002b, p. 147)

'...[D]eaths in custody are high and are increasing'. (House of Lords House of Commons Joint Committee on Human Rights, 2004a, p.3)

Introduction

In the 14 month period between July 1990 and September 1991, three children aged 15, Jeffrey Horler, Philip Knight and Craig Walsh and a fourth child,

Simon Willerton aged 17, died in penal custody in England and Wales. Naturally concern was expressed by a wide range of statutory agencies and non-governmental organisations. Accordingly, the Government and the Prison Service provided various assurances that the care of children in penal custody would be given urgent attention. Since that time, and up to the end of January 2005, a further 24 children have similarly died: Andrew Batey, aged 17; Mark Dade, aged 16; David Dennis, aged 17; Kirk Edwards, aged 17; Chris Greenaway, aged 16; Philip Griffin, aged 17; Kevin Henson, aged 17; Anthony Howarth, aged 17; Kevin Jacobs, aged 16; John Keyworth, aged 17; Patrick Murphy, aged 16; Gareth Myatt, aged 15; Gareth Price, aged 16; Ian Powell, aged 17; Anthony Redding, aged 16; Adam Rickwood, aged 14; Colin Scarborough, aged 17; Joseph Scholes, aged 16; Joseph Stanley, aged 17; David Stewart, aged 17; Lee Wagstaff, aged 17; Mark Weldrand, aged 16; Nicholas Whelan, aged 16 and Ryan Winter, aged 17. In total, 28 children have died in penal custody over a period of 15 years: an average of two child deaths every year, all but two self-inflicted.

Each and all of these deaths relate to boys. Given that statistical data affirms that female prisoners are five times more likely to harm themselves than male detainees, and that all young prisoners are more inclined to self-harm than their older counterparts (The Howard League for Penal Reform, 2001b, p. 4), the mono-gendered nature of child deaths in penal custody is seemingly anomalous. Other than noting that the overwhelming majority of the child prisoner population comprises boys, however, accounting for such an anomaly is beyond the reach of this book.

During the same period of time – and in addition to the 28 child deaths – literally thousands of children (boys and girls) have harmed themselves in penal custody. According to the Howard League for Penal Reform (2005, p.22), for example, '1,659 incidents of self-injury or attempted suicide by juveniles in prisons were recorded from 1998 to 2002'. As is noted later, it is more difficult to measure and quantify the less tangible detrimental impact – physical, psychological, emotional hurt – that penal custody inflicts on children but the depressing reality, given its increasing use, is that further death, harm and damage will almost certainly follow.

Case summaries: Philip Knight, Craig Walsh and Jeffrey Horler

Philip Knight: Died July 12 1990 aged 15 years

Philip had an unsettled family background and he was taken into the care of the Local Authority when he was 13 years old. He was a troubled child who regularly truanted school and ran away from his care placements in order to return to the family home. On one absconding episode Philip took a handbag from a table in a cafeteria. It was an impulsive and opportunistic theft. Unbeknown to Philip, however, the handbag contained a substantial amount of money: he had inadvertently committed a serious offence. Having appeared in court Philip was granted bail and returned to the Children's Home. Soon after his return Philip slashed his wrists whereupon the Social Services Department moved him to another care placement. As his distress accumulated his behaviour deteriorated. Seemingly unable to manage Philip, Social Services applied to the court for a 'Certificate of Unruly Character' and he was placed in Her Majesty's Prison Swansea.

The Social Services Department verbally notified the Police that Philip was a vulnerable child and a form was duly completed alerting the prison that he had 'suicidal tendencies' (Coles and Ward, 1994, p. 134). Social Services also provided similar verbal notice directly to prison personnel. Accordingly, an oral instruction was issued within the prison requiring staff to observe Philip more closely than was usual practice and to place him in a cell with another young prisoner. Within two days Philip had an altercation with his 'cell mate' and he erected a barricade for which he 'was placed in a single cell in the punishment block' (*ibid*, p. 134). A 'Personal Officer' was assigned to Philip, although it later transpired that the officer was unaware of the concerns that had been raised in terms of the boy's vulnerability and risk. At Philip's inquest the same officer gave evidence during which he explained that strained staffing levels and lack of time meant that the 'Personal Officer' scheme was rendered ineffective at Swansea Prison.

On July 6, following seven days in solitary confinement, Philip cut deeply into his left wrist. On being transferred to the prison hospital he told a prison officer that he wanted to die and this was formally recorded using the Prison Service F210 form. However, having examined Philip, the prison doctor did not consider the boy to be suicidal. Instead, the doctor interpreted Philip's self inflicted injury to be an 'expression of anger and resentment' (Inquest testimony cited in Coles and Ward, 1994, p. 134). Philip was placed in a strip cell dressed only in a canvas garment. The inquest testimonies of the prison doctor, the chaplain and other officers confirmed that Philip was perceived to be a discipline and control problem whose self-injury was a manipulative expression of attention seeking. The doctor reported that he could not recall whether he had read the F210 documentation (*ibid*, p. 134).

On July 12 Philip appeared in Court in respect of the offence of theft. He expected to be transferred to a specialist secure unit for juveniles only to learn that no such placement was available. He was returned to Swansea Prison. Later the same day Philip Knight, a seriously distressed 15 year old boy, hanged himself from his cell bars and died.

Craig Walsh: Died October 26 1990 aged 15 years

Craig spent much of his short life in residential care, although the very notion of 'care' was something of a misnomer. Whilst being 'looked after' by Staffordshire Social Services Department Craig was reportedly exposed to the abusive practices that became known as 'Pindown' (Moore and Taggart, 1991, p. 8). 'Pindown' was a system in which 'control was exercised over children through a regime of quasi-behaviour modification which deprived them of their liberty and subjected them to social isolation, humiliation and oppression' (Kahan, 1994, pp. 46-7). Not surprisingly perhaps, and not unlike Philip Knight, Craig regularly absconded from his 'care' placements. Ultimately, Craig was regarded as being so distressed that he was placed at Glenthorne Youth Treatment Centre in Birmingham, a specialist residential resource managed directly by the Department of Health. Craig absconded from Glenthorne too, however, and whilst 'on the run' he held his Aunt at knife point and took money from her, an offence for which he was sent to Her Majesty's Young Offender Institution Glen Parva.

Craig's mother reported that she had seen 'suicide risk' written across the top of his prison papers and such was the concern, that efforts where being made to transfer him out of the prison system and back to a secure placement at Glenthorne (Moore and Taggart, 1991, p. 8). In the meantime, however, Craig was detained in solitary confinement for extended periods. Towards the end of October 1990 an alternative placement was eventually found for Craig and he was scheduled to move back to Glenthorne on October 27. Prison Officers subsequently reported that he appeared to be happy and excited about returning to Glenthorne. On October 26, however, Craig was kept isolated in a double cell for over 8 hours. On what was to be – and indeed was – his final day in prison, 15 year old Craig Walsh took his own life by hanging from a prison bedstead.

At the inquest into Craig's death the Home Office, prison personnel and social services staff were each legally represented. Craig's family had no legal representation. The inquest was completed with indecent haste and the entire proceedings were concluded within an hour. Moore and Taggart (1991, p.8) raise a range of pressing questions: 'Why did he die? Was Glen Parva's care lacking? Was it the effects of 8 hours isolation? Was he afraid to go to Glenthorne? Was he psychologically damaged by "Pindown" and the care system?' The cursory nature of the inquest failed inevitably to provide any conclusive answers.

Jeffrey Horler: Died September 22 1991 aged 15 years

Jeffrey was born in Great Yarmouth on May 13, 1976. Social Services had periodic involvement with Jeffrey's family for many years and in 1990, aged 14 years, he was received into care and placed with foster parents. After a period Jeffrey returned to live with his mother. This was not to be the only occasion that Jeffrey was 'looked after', however, and Social Services retained ongoing contact with him via an allocated Social Worker.

Like many children who spend periods of time in Local Authority care, Jeffrey was troubled and periodically troublesome. He had committed low-level offences and had been the subject of community disposals. In August 1991, however, the Great Yarmouth Juvenile Court sentenced him to four months Youth Custody for setting fire to an old smokehouse. This was Jeffrey's first and last custodial sentence.

At the time that Jeffrey was sentenced to custody there was no penal institution in Norfolk that could legally detain a boy of such a young age. Accordingly, Jeffrey was sent to the biggest juvenile prison in Western Europe at Her Majesty's Young Offender Institution Feltham, some 200 miles from his home area. Jeffrey did not receive a single visit whilst he was at Feltham. His mother made contact by telephone on two occasions and he exchanged letters with his family and a neighbour. Jeffrey's mother, with other children to care for, could not afford to visit him and she was never informed that she was eligible to claim financial assistance for visiting (The Howard League for Penal Reform, 1993a, p. 9).

On August 26 Jeffrey's grandmother died, although he was not notified of this until days later. On August 31 a prison officer found him sobbing in his cell. Jeffrey explained that he wanted to buy flowers and attend his grandmother's funeral. A senior prison officer contacted Norfolk Social Services Department to inform them that, given the circumstances, an exception could be made to normal Young Offender Institution rules in order to allow Jeffrey to attend the funeral. This simply required Social Services to make appropriate transport and escort arrangements but they decided not to do so. Jeffrey's allocated Social Worker later explained that:

'We considered the effect on Jeffrey. We knew him well and we believed that although he might well be upset about his grandmother's death, missing the funeral would not have a very great effect on him. We also considered the obvious practical difficulties – it is nearly 200 miles from Yarmouth to Feltham... There was also the cost that had to be considered'. (Cited in The Howard League for Penal Reform, 1993a, p. 9).

At no stage did Social Services staff actually speak to Jeffrey to assess his emotional state in relation to his grandmother's death. Just three weeks later he was found hanging from the bars of his cell. Jeffrey Horler died on September 22, 1991 aged 15 years.

During 1992-93 Anthony Scrivener QC chaired an inquiry into 'Suicides at Feltham' commissioned by the Howard League for Penal Reform to which INQUEST provided detailed evidence derived from its extensive casework. Reflecting on Jeffrey's death Scrivener reported that:

> 'Mrs Horler told the inquiry that there was no expectation of a custodial sentence prior to Jeffrey's hearing and believed that the court reacted badly to her statement that she could not afford to pay any more fines. Whether or not this is the case, the trauma for a 15 year old being locked in a cell for most of the day was compounded by the emotional isolation the shift to Feltham involved... the offences could not be described as the most serious... With the benefit of hindsight and a fuller appreciation of the facts it can be seen that a custodial sentence had a disastrous consequence for Jeffrey. Although he had few things of a positive nature to build upon in his life, he had one important connection. He seems to have had a firm link with his family... The inevitable consequence of the sentence was to send him 200 miles away from his family. He was removed from whatever security this connection gave him and left to cope with the hostile environment of Feltham on his own'. (Cited in The Howard League for Penal Reform, 1993a, p. 27)

Jeffrey was the third 15 year old boy to take his life in prison in just over a year.

Philip, Craig and Jeffrey were children with much in common. Each was aged 15, had troubled backgrounds necessitating the formal interventions of Social Services and had each been 'looked after' away from home. They had been damaged in the infrastructure of everyday life and, in many respects, had been failed by adults and professional agencies alike. Although each· committed what might be regarded as a single 'serious offence', none could reasonably be described as a prolific and/or persistent offender and none posed any sustained danger to the community at large. They were manifestly vulnerable children and, on entering penal custody, the relevant authorities were notified of the 'risks'. Communication blockages and breakdown were evident in each case and, in particular, nobody seemed to 'hear' the children themselves. They were inappropriately placed in penal custody and prison officers were unable to meet their needs and/or to keep them safe. The specific responses of the penal institutions, ostensibly implemented as special safety measures, were more akin to punishment and isolation. Each child managed to survive penal custody for a relatively short period of time but, ultimately, each was discharged dead.

The enduring nature of child deaths in penal custody

'The headlines are stark. This year, while the suicide rate in the community as a whole has been falling, the rate in prisons has increased'. (Her Majesty's Chief Inspector of Prisons, 2004b, p.3)

This is the introductory sentence in the Chief Inspector of Prisons Annual Report in 2004. Of all the issues that might have been highlighted, the one at the forefront of her mind was prisoner suicides. This is no aberration however, no peculiarity of a particular year. Death, including the deaths of children, comprises a stubbornly persistent feature of penal custody. The 'headlines' may well have been 'stark' in 2003-04, but the longer history of child deaths in penal custody is starker still. This book is primarily concerned with the period July 1990 – January 2005 and, throughout this time, the enduring nature of deaths in penal custody in general, and child/youth deaths in particular, can be traced through the pages of INQUEST's Annual Reports:

'Deaths in custody... featured prominently during this period due to the scandalous number of prison suicides – 48 in 1989, 51 in 1990... The increase in deaths of young people in custody is a matter of serious concern'. (INQUEST, 1990, pp. 2-3)

'The number of self-inflicted deaths and self-mutilations in prison continues to be disturbingly high... As long as children are sent to prison they will continue to die. It is scandalous that the prison authorities continue with this policy'. (INQUEST, 1992, p. 5)

'In 1992, there were 77 deaths in British prisons... Already in 1993, 33 people have killed themselves. There is also disturbingly high incidents of self injury. If Michael Howard's [the Home Secretary] suggestions regarding building new prisons, stricter regimes and more custodial sentences, especially for younger people, are implemented, this figure is destined to increase'. (INQUEST, 1993, p. 7)

'... [I]n 1994 there was a 20 per cent increase in self-inflicted deaths in prison... There has been an appalling increase in youth deaths – with 1994 witnessing the highest figure in five years... Inquests into youth deaths this year reveal a pattern of repeated failure with vital lessons not learnt about how to prevent more loss of life in the future'. (INQUEST, 1994, p. 5)

'There were 64 self-inflicted deaths in prison in 1996 – the highest figure since INQUEST's formation. Twelve of these were young men'. (INQUEST, 1996, p. 9)

'In monitoring all deaths in prison... we remain concerned about... the increase in the number of deaths of... young prisoners'. (INQUEST, 1999, p. 14)

'For many years INQUEST has expressed concerns regarding the care of young prisoners and whether Young Offender Institutions can provide the level of care these vulnerable young people need. INQUEST has had long-standing concerns regarding the ever-increasing number of youth deaths in prison'. (INQUEST, 2000, p. 9)

'INQUEST is appalled that yet again young people and children continue to die whilst in HM Young Offenders Institutions. In what looks like a year in which a record number of young people (21 years old and below) have been found dead in HMYOIs there have also been three children aged 16 who have been found hanging in their cells'. (INQUEST, 2001, p. 15)

'During 2003 the issue of prison deaths was high on our agenda due to the further surge in the prison population and the number of self-inflicted deaths'. (INQUEST, 2003a, p.7)

'... the deaths of children and young people in custody... has been a priority area of work during 2004'. (INQUEST, 2004a)

The message that comes across, therefore, is that death, harm and damage is not only a permanent feature of penal custody but also, with the passage of time, it has become more common. Indeed, a major thematic review of prison suicides concluded that: 'the rate of self inflicted deaths in prison more than doubled between 1982 and 1998... [and] the increase... is larger than would be expected from the rise in the prisoner population' (Her Majesty's Chief Inspector of Prisons, 1999b, p. 11). Furthermore, as previously noted, self-harm has also become increasingly widespread in penal custody over the last decade or more. It is an everyday feature of prison life (Medlicott, 2001, p. 19) and it is 'particularly prevalent in the 15-25 years age range' (Her Majesty's Chief Inspector of Prisons, 1999b, para. 5.16).

Measuring death, harm and damage

'I think that when the door closes and there is no-one else around, the bravado goes and they realise that they are just children. The thought of me being locked up alone when I was 15, it would have scared the hell out of me. That's when they become frightened'. (Prison Officer, cited in Goldson, 2002b, p. 128)

'I was really scared in my pad... I was lying on my bed proper scared thinking I don't want to go out there in the morning, I don't want to go out at all'. (Child prisoner aged 15 years, cited in Goldson, 2002b, p. 142)

If measuring death in penal custody is readily quantifiable, measuring harm and damage is far more difficult. Whilst the recorded evidence suggests that the incidence of self-harm in prisons in England and Wales has increased substantially over the last decade or more (Liebling, 1996; Neal, 1996; McHugh and Snow, 2000; Prison Reform Trust, 2004a), this tells only part of the story. Indeed, such official statistics fail to provide an accurate measure of the true extent of self-harm in prisons, much of which continues to go unrecorded (Liebling and Krarup, 1993; Howard League, 1999; Medlicott, 2001; INQUEST, 2004b).

Furthermore, in order to fully comprehend death, harm and damage in penal custody it is necessary to look beyond the purely *quantifiable* and *quantitative* and to engage also with the infinitely more complex *qualitative* dimension. In this respect our knowledge is severely limited not least because, as Medlicott (2001, p. 5) observes: 'those who could best illuminate causation are dead'. Indeed, it is nearly impossible to comprehensively measure the damage that penal custody imposes. Incidents of self-harm might be counted and statistics collated but such data are profoundly limited. The data not only bypass the unrecorded as already noted, but they also fail to capture the real essence, the depth of pain, that motivates child prisoners to turn in on themselves, to self-harm and/or to take life. In this sense, perhaps imagination is our most incisive and appreciative research method. A deeper understanding might be achieved, therefore, by reflecting on what passes through a child's mind in prison; what drives a child to deliberate self-harm and, ultimately, how desperate a child must become before they are left feeling that death is preferable to life.

Despite the methodological limitations and the deficiencies of official data, however, the available statistics present a harrowing picture of death, harm and damage. As noted earlier, multiple disadvantage, personal trauma, fear, loneliness, anxiety, uncertainty, injustice, powerlessnes, bullying, abuse and violation are the common characteristics of child prisoners. By any measure they are a profoundly vulnerable group (Goldson, 2002b). Within a context of penal expansion and with increasing numbers of children entering custody, therefore, they continue to die. More generally, 21,760 incidents of self-harm were reported in prisons between 1998 and 2002 (INQUEST, 2004b) and the numbers continue to rise. There was a 30 per cent increase in such incidents in 2003 (Her Majesty's Chief Inspector of Prisons, 2004b, p.13) and in 2004 17,678 cases were reported (Her Majesty's Chief Inspector of Prisons, 2005, p.16). Whilst it should be acknowledged that a heightened sensitivity to self-harm, together with more effective methods of recording, may well impose an inflationary effect, the fact remains that penal custody is routinely damaging and, not infrequently, fatally so. Despite constant policy reform and practice experimentation towards the goal of 'safer custody', the 'jail-house', however it is configured, remains a dangerous place for children.

Towards 'Safer Custody'? Before and beyond Tumin and Ramsbotham

'The Prisons Strategy Board should introduce suicide prevention strategies for... young prisoners which are based on the different needs of this group'. (Her Majesty's Chief Inspector of Prisons, 1999b, para. 8.11)

'In terms of a policy... it may be positively unhelpful to label selected prisoners as "vulnerable", thereby implicitly characterising the rest as invulnerable'. (Medlicott, 2001, p.58)

Contemporary policy and practice that aims to secure 'safer custody' can be traced back to the first Prison Service Circular Instruction in 1973 (McHugh and Snow, 2000). This laid the foundations upon which subsequent 'suicide prevention' efforts have rested. The Instruction served not only to heighten awareness and sharpen the focus of attention in general terms; it also emphasised the specific significance of 'risk factors', effective communication, reception assessments and the requirement for support and care. In many respects the 1973 Instruction set the agenda around which subsequent reforms have developed.

Further Circular Instructions, issued in 1983, proposed the formation of 'management groups' in prisons to develop, co-ordinate and implement suicide prevention policies and practices. The same Instructions reiterated the significance of reception procedures, staff awareness, referral protocols, medical assessments and appropriate recording and communication. Suicide and self-harm were essentially 'medicalised' and this emphasis was reinforced by a review led by Her Majesty's Chief Inspector of Prisons and published in 1984 (Home Office, 1984). The review conceptualised suicide and self-harm primarily as medical issues, it placed the principal responsibility for prevention with the Medical Officer and it affirmed the importance of screening, assessment, referral and treatment.

In 1987 revised 'suicide prevention' procedures came into effect in the Prison Service. 'The high suicide rate continued' (Her Majesty's Chief Inspector of Prisons, 1999b, para. 5.1), however, and the new procedures were soon followed by the publication of a further Circular Instruction on the 'Prevention of Suicide and Self-Injury' in 1989 (C.I. 20/89). The Instruction set out four principal targets:

- To improve the identification of potentially suicidal prisoners by implementing systematic methods of medical assessment at reception.
- To assist particularly vulnerable prisoners to recover from crisis through location in the prison hospital or 'some other suitable place', that might include a shared cell or placement in an 'unfurnished cell' in 'protective clothing' (strip conditions).
- To reduce the opportunities for suicide without impeding the 'quality of life' for prisoners.
- To establish a 'Suicide Prevention Management Group' (SPMG) in order to ensure that all staff are aware of the problem of prisoner suicide and how best to prevent its occurrence.

The combined effect of these targets included:

- A sharper focus on 'assessment' and the requirement that all prisoners were to be seen by a doctor within 24 hours of their arrival; screening for identified 'risk indicators' (in particular, previous incidents of self-harm, mental ill-health and/or history of psychiatric problems, substance misuse, certain offence categories and social isolation).
- The introduction of specific documentation for the purposes of recording assessments and outlining treatment/management plans (Medical Officers were made wholly responsible for assessing risk and defining appropriate responses).

- More concerted efforts to provide conditions facilitating support and interaction with staff, family, prison visitors and, where possible, Samaritans.

The primary emphasis, therefore, retained focus on the medical/psychiatric and procedural. Prisoners assessed as suicidal and/or at risk of self-harm, were conceptualised as pathological. The 'solution' was found primarily in more rigorously applied processes of assessment and monitoring. There was little official attention paid to the 'social' dimensions of death, harm and damage in penal custody; the pain of confinement; the corrosive impact of conditions and treatment and the intrinsic deleterious nature of the prison environment itself (Sim, 1990; Ryan, 1996).

In February 1990, the Home Secretary, David Waddington, announced another review that was to be conducted by Her Majesty's Chief Inspector of Prisons, Sir Stephen Tumin. Tumin was asked to:

'... review the effectiveness of the current policy and procedures for the prevention of suicide and self-harm in Prison Service establishments in England and Wales, with particular reference to mentally disturbed prisoners; and to make recommendations'. (Cited in Her Majesty's Chief Inspector of Prisons, 1999b, para. 5.1)

Tumin's report was published in December 1990 (Her Majesty's Chief Inspector of Prisons, 1990) and it contained 123 recommendations. (During the very same period that the report was being prepared Philip Knight, Craig Walsh and Simon Willerton each lost their lives in penal custody). The report was critical, at least in part, of the 1989 Circular Instruction, claiming that it was overly concerned with 'formal procedures', as distinct from 'encouraging proper attitudes towards inmates' (*ibid*, para. 2.03) as a central part of a general philosophy of prisoner care. It also took issue with previous policies, practices and procedures that treated 'self-inflicted death as exclusively a medical problem' (*ibid*, para. 2.07). Tumin observed that the majority of people who took their own lives in prison custody were not mentally disordered as defined by statute and that suicide prevention was essentially a 'social' as distinct from a 'medical' issue. Whilst mental distress is commonplace in penal custody – and in many respects is an inevitable product of penal regimes – Her Majesty's Chief Inspector of Prisons noted that:

'Current Prison Department policy fails to communicate the social dimension to self-harm and self-inflicted death. It does not stress sufficiently the significance of the environment in which prisoners... are expected to live'. (*ibid*, para. 1.08)

After the publication of Sir Stephen Tumin's report, the Prison Service established the 'Suicide Awareness Support Unit' in 1991, dedicated to developing and communicating national strategy, disseminating research and good practice and providing advice and support to local 'Suicide Prevention Management Groups'. Furthermore, a range of 'policies on suicide awareness and guidance from the Prison Service mushroomed' (The Howard League for Penal Reform, 1993b, p. 20). A guidance pack, 'Caring for the Suicidal in Custody', was published in 1992, followed by an information paper, 'The Way Forward', published later the same year. An 'Instruction to Governors' (1/94) was issued in 1994, accompanied by a comprehensive strategy document 'Guide to Policy and Procedures – Caring for the Suicidal in Custody'. The main features of the 1994 strategy included:

• Greater responsibility for *all* prison staff in caring for prisoners adjudged to be suicidal.
• A move away from an exclusive reliance on health care staff.
• The introduction of a new form – F2052SH – for assessing and communicating information in respect of prisoners considered to be 'at risk'.
• Greater involvement of the Samaritans and the development of 'Listener Schemes'.

Finally, in December 1997, the Minister for Prisons, Joyce Quinn, asked Sir David Ramsbotham, Her Majesty's Chief Inspector of Prisons, to 'carry out a thematic review of Suicide and Self-Harm in Prison Service establishments in England and Wales, to follow up that undertaken by [his] predecessor, Sir Stephen Tumin in 1990' (Her Majesty's Chief Inspector of Prisons, 1999b, p. 3). The report, published in 1999 and running to 136 pages, observed that 'although policies were in place across the Prison Service, there was little differentiation within them between the needs of different types of prisoner' (*ibid*, para. 5.13). In particular, attention was drawn to child and young prisoners whose specific needs and unique circumstances previously had been overlooked.

On one level progress has been made, both in respect of researching death, harm and damage in penal custody and in shaping more responsive policies, practices and procedures. The exclusively medical/psychiatric and quantitative emphasis that characterised earlier research, primarily focussing upon retrospective analyses of individual cases and calculating trends (see for example, Topp, 1979; Philips, 1986; Dooley, 1990), has been (at least partially) displaced by more 'socially' grounded and qualitative approaches that appreciate the fundamental significance of 'prison place' (see, for example: Liebling, 2004). Similarly, developments in policy recognising the specific circumstances of child prisoners and emphasising more holistic constructions of the 'healthy prison' and 'safer custody', have ostensibly moved beyond crude genericism and mechanistic procedures.

On another level, however, progress such as it is has failed to return positive 'results'. As already noted, death, harm and damage continues to prevail and in the same way that the concluding decade of the twentieth century witnessed the death of children in penal custody, the opening decade of the twenty first century has been similarly stained.

Case summaries: Anthony Redding and Kevin Jacobs

Anthony Redding: Died February 15 2001 aged 16 years

Anthony was sent to Her Majesty's Young Offender Institution Brinsford near Wolverhampton on January 25, 2001, having been sentenced to a four month Detention and Training Order for car-related offences. By any definition Anthony was a vulnerable child. His parents had removed him from school after he had been systematically targetted by bullies. Moreover, Anthony knew what to expect from prison and such knowledge filled him with dread. He had served a two month sentence in 2000 during which time he was re-acquainted with bullying. Equally, the Prison Service and related professional agencies knew what to expect from Anthony. He had struggled with his first experience of penal custody and he had seriously self-harmed. The Youth Offending Service in Coventry, his home city, had notified the court of Anthony's previous self-harming behaviour. Such concern was soon confirmed. No sooner had the second custodial sentence been imposed when Anthony attempted to hang himself with shoe laces in the cellular escort vehicle that took him to prison. .

On arriving at Brinsford Anthony was placed in the Health Care Centre and subjected to regular checks at 15 minute intervals under 'Suicide Watch' procedures. Despite relatively intensive monitoring and surveillance, Anthony attempted to strangle himself using a blanket. He consistently expressed high levels of anxiety. Despite this, and the efforts of the Youth Offending Service to have him transferred to a Local Authority Secure Children's Home, Anthony was soon moved to 'normal location' and placed in a shared prison cell. At the first opportunity, and 'within minutes of being left alone while his cell mate went to an interview, he tried to hang himself' (Children's Rights Alliance for England, 2002, p. 66).

Anthony was immediately relocated back to the Health Care Centre. Within less than a week however, and against his stated wishes, he was returned to the prison wing, this time in a single cell. The Health Care staff advised that he should be checked at frequent intervals. On February 14, a Prison Officer, an hour and ten minutes after the last check, found Anthony hanging from the bars in his cell. He was transferred to a local hospital but never regained consciousness. On the evening of February 15, 2001, just three weeks after being sent back to prison, Anthony Redding, aged 16 years, was pronounced dead.

Kevin Jacobs: Died September 29 2001 aged 16 years

Kevin had been in Local Authority care from an early age. His experience of the 'care' system was not positive. He was sexually violated and abused whilst being 'looked after' and 'suffered a horrendous history of institutional neglect' (INQUEST, 2002, p. 1). On July 3, 2001, whilst the subject of a statutory Care Order and the responsibility of Lambeth Social Services Department, Kevin was remanded to Her Majesty's Young Offender Institution Feltham. Just over two weeks later, on July 19 2001, he was sentenced to a six month Detention and Training Order to be served at Feltham.

All of the professionals who came into contact with Kevin concurred that he was a vulnerable child with manifest needs. Despite this, however, together with a wealth of evidence confirming his distress, disturbed behaviour and history of self-harm, he continued to be held in prison custody rather than being transferred to a more appropriate placement within a local authority secure children's home or hospital setting. Moreover, as time passed Kevin became even more anxious about his immediate future. He had not been told where he would be accommodated once discharged from prison. He was literally dependent upon Lambeth Social Services Department and yet he had been given indications that his place at the Children's Home in Guilford, where he had lived prior to being sent to prison, had been foreclosed without any alternative arrangements in place. Kevin, like many children with a history of Local Authority 'care', was frightened at the prospect of being abandoned and left to struggle with the isolation and loneliness that bed-and-breakfast accommodation brings. He made a serious attempt to hang himself on September 14, 2001,

On September 26 torn sheets, together with a ligature hook, were found under the bed in Kevin's cell. Prison staff recorded that they were 'extremely concerned about his safety' (Children's Rights Alliance for England, 2002 p. 66). Kevin was moved to the Health Care Centre whereupon he described experiencing vivid flashbacks to periods when he had been sexually abused and, in a state of high anxiety and distress, he damaged his cell. Accordingly he was placed in a 'low-stimulus' cell overnight, where he was checked every fifteen minutes.

On the morning of September 27 Kevin was directly returned to his cell on the prison wing and was checked every hour. The following day Kevin received a visit from his Social Worker during which he was notified that he would not be returning to his former children's home in Guilford. That was the last time a representative of Social Services, Kevin's legal parents, saw him alive. In the early hours of September 29 2001 Kevin Jacobs was found hanging from the bars in his cell. He was 16 years old.

Safer still? Placement, assessment and protection

'Reducing prisoner self-inflicted deaths and managing self-harm is a key priority for Ministers and the Prison Service. A proactive three-year strategy to develop policies and practices to reduce prisoner suicide and manage self-harm in prisons was announced by the then Home Secretary, Jack Straw, and was implemented from April 2001'. (Her Majesty's Prison Service, 2004, para. 2.1)

'... [Y]oung people should be placed in accommodation, which most effectively meets their needs and the risk of harm that they pose to themselves and others. The accommodation should be appropriate for their age, emotional maturity and level of vulnerability... placements for remanded and sentenced juveniles should be based on a comprehensive assessment of their needs and risks completed to defined national standards'. (Youth Justice Board, 1998, pp. 26-27)

In recent years a Ministerial 'Roundtable' on 'Suicide in Prisons' has convened. It is chaired by the Government Minister for Prisons and Probation and its membership includes: Her Majesty's Chief Inspector of Prisons; The Howard League for Penal Reform; INQUEST; Prison Health (the partnership between the Prison Service and the Department of Health); The Prison Reform Trust; The Prisons and Probation Ombudsman; The Samaritans and The Youth Justice Board for England and Wales. Alongside the 'Roundtable', a range of additional measures have been implemented in an effort to minimise the likelihood of death, harm and damage in penal custody. These measures are not specifically designed with child prisoners in mind and they have a generic application across the prison system. They include:

- The establishment, in April 2001, of the 'Safer Custody Group' in order to deliver a 'Safer Custody Strategy'.
- The publication, in December 2001, of the government's strategy for developing mental health services in prisons, entitled 'Changing the Outlook: A Strategy for Developing and Modernising Mental Health Services in Prisons'.
- The publication, in November 2002, of a new Prison Service Order (PSO 2700) entitled 'Suicide and Self-Harm Prevention', which replaced previous 'guidance' with 'mandatory requirements'.
- The development of 'violence reduction strategies' to counter inter-prisoner violence and particularly bullying in prisons.
- The appointment of 'Suicide Prevention Co-ordinators' (SPCs) in prisons.
- The creation of projects to develop 'safer' prison design, including 'safer cells'.
- The introduction of initiatives aimed to improve pre-reception, reception and induction processes in prisons including more effective and thorough health care screening.
- The development of policies, practices and procedures to facilitate more effective inter-agency and intra-agency communication and information exchange.
- The wider application of Samaritans projects and 'Listener' schemes within prisons.
- The delivery of additional staff training, including suicide and self-harm 'awareness courses' for Prison Service personnel.

With specific regard to child prisoners, perhaps the most significant reform of recent times has been the establishment of a new executive non-departmental public body, the Youth Justice Board for England and Wales (YJB). The YJB was given statutory effect by the Crime and Disorder Act 1998 and its principal responsibilities include advising the Home Secretary on the operation of the youth justice system, monitoring performance, establishing standards and supporting new practice initiatives. Soon after the establishment of the Board, it turned its attention to the question of children in penal custody, advising the Home Secretary that: 'there is clear evidence that the current arrangements for juvenile secure facilities are highly unsatisfactory' (Youth Justice Board, 1998, p.12). Such observations echoed authoritative findings from previously published reports. In particular, both the Department of Health's 'Children's Safeguards Review' (Utting, 1997) and the 'Thematic Review of Young Prisoners' conducted by Her Majesty's Chief Inspector of Prisons (1997), had each raised serious concerns about the conditions and treatment endured by children in prisons. Building on such publications, therefore, and within the context of the wider efforts being made to minimise the likelihood of child death, harm and damage in penal custody, the YJB has endeavoured, along with its other duties, to apply the 'safer custody' agenda to the 'juvenile secure estate'.

The Youth Justice Board has implemented a number of practical 'safer custody' measures including funding for 24 hour healthcare, the provision of 'First Night' packs, the commissioning of a regular survey of children in Young Offender Institutions and the commissioning of advocacy services for child prisoners. More generally, emphasis has focussed upon the questions of placement, assessment and protection.

Placement

Essentially the YJB introduced a business model and a contracting culture into the realm of penal custody. Institutions that comprise the 'juvenile secure estate' had service 'standards' imposed upon them, were classified as 'authorised' or 'accredited', must operate and 'deliver' in accordance with 'contracting conditions' and are expected to provide 'placements' that are 'purchased' or 'commissioned' (Youth Justice Board, 1998). The Board issued generic *National Standards for Youth Justice* (Youth Justice Board, 2000a and 2004b) and, more specifically, it:

• Established a partnership arrangement with the Prison Service operationalised through 'Service Delivery Agreements' with each of the 17 Young Offender Institutions within the 'under 18 estate' (Hughes and Thompson, 2000).
• Settled arrangements with the Home Office to manage contracts with the Secure Training Centres (private jails for children).
• Issued a 'Generic Service Specification' for Local Authority Secure Children's Homes together with a 'Service Credit Scheme' tailored to each individual unit.
• Attached 'Compliance Monitors' to each of the contracted institutions who, in turn, report to 'Compliance Managers' with regard to service performance.

In sum, in order to fulfil its 'commissioning' functions and operationalise its 'contracting' arrangements, the YJB, in consultation with the Home Office and the Department of Health, established 'purchasing agreements' with 'placement providers', based upon agreed costings and service specifications and located within a 'comprehensive performance monitoring framework' (Youth Justice Board, 2004a, p.5). Ostensibly this provides rationality within which the YJB is able to 'purchase' 'placements' from the 'providers' (the Prison Service, the Local Authority Secure Children's Homes and the privately managed Secure Training Centres), allowing it to place children in 'an establishment that can most effectively manage their identified needs and risk factors' (Youth Justice Board, 2004c, para. 2).

To operationalise this process, the YJB has established a centralised national 'Placements Team' that takes the strategic overview of the contracted placements within the 'Juvenile Secure Estate' and, in conjunction with the locally based Youth Offending Teams, allocates 'places' accordingly. Managing the 'supply' of penal custody without having control over the 'demand' side poses formidable challenges, however. Furthermore, within the contemporary context of penal expansion in which the overwhelming majority of 'places' are located within the Prison Service sector, the 'placement' options available to the YJB, particularly in respect of the the non-prison sector, are severely restricted. Despite the reform effort, therefore, the capacity of the YJB to exercise informed discretion and/or to 'place' children appropriately, is fundamentally circumscribed. In fact the reality is that 'placements' are ultimately governed by availability, supply and cost and, accordingly, the placements process is determined by pragmatism and expediency as distinct from qualitative welfare-based judgements regarding children's respective needs and risks (Goldson, 2002b; Youth Justice Board 2004a).

Assessment

If the 'placements' system is marred by operational imperfections, it follows that carefully executed 'risk assessments' are, by definition, extremely important. Indeed, one of the principal ways through which the Prison Service and the YJB have attempted to minimise the likelihood of child deaths, harm and damage in penal custody is by developing more detailed 'assessment' policies, practices and procedures. Since its inception, the YJB has emphasised consistently the importance of a continuous or 'joined-up' process of assessment for children sent to penal custody:

> 'When young people are about to enter [penal custody] there should be a rigorous, comprehensive and standard assessment of their... needs... This work should start when a YOT member identifies a need to find a placement and should continue in the institution'. (Youth Justice Board, 1998, pp. 17-18)

The process of assessment that has developed involves contributions from various agencies and, in its complete form, it comprises at least seven discrete but inter-connected stages. Each stage is (in theory) accompanied by specific documentation:

- First, the *Youth Justice Board Placement Alert Form* (PL05) must be completed by Youth Offending Teams and transmitted to the YJB Placement's Team in advance of court hearings: 'ideally this should be no later than the day before the court appearance' (Youth Justice Board, 2004d, para. 1), in respect of every child for whom a custodial sentence and/or penal remand is anticipated. If the Youth Offending Team has assessed the child as vulnerable 'supporting documents must [also] be sent with the completed form to the placement team' (*ibid*, para. 2)

- Second, the *Asset* form is the standard 'assessment tool'. It is a detailed form that is designed to be completed in respect of *each child* who comes into contact with the youth justice system. With regard to child prisoners the form has a dual purpose. First, it is employed to assess the child's vulnerability or, more specifically, the 'risk' that they might present to themselves. Second, it is also intended to be used to assess the 'risk' that the child might pose to others. The 'joined-up' nature of assessment is such, that the Asset form must be sent to the Youth Justice Board Placement's Team in order to alert personnel of any perceived 'risks' and/or 'vulnerabilities' and, it is also meant to travel with every child who enters penal custody in order to inform staff at the point of arrival/reception.

- Third, a *Risk of Serious Harm Assessment* must be completed if the Asset form indicates that there is some prospect of the child seriously harming themselves or others. In cases where the YOT completes such an assessment it is required to share the information with other relevant agencies (Youth Justice Board, 2004b, Standard 4).

- Fourth, the *Post-Court Report* (PCR) is designed to provide essential information for custodial facilities, to be completed by YOT staff in respect of each child remanded or sentenced to penal custody. The PCR requires the YOT worker to include information on the child's personal and family details; any special needs the child may have with regard to communication; the child's health status including treatment that may be urgently required in respect of substance misuse; the risk of harm that the child may pose to others; the child's vulnerability; and relevant additional information.

- Fifth, the *Prisoner Escort Record* (PER) is meant to be completed by 'prisoner escorts' in all cases when children are escorted from Court to penal custody. The PER form requires the escort to assess the child's risk (either to self or others) and three 'tick-box' columns – entitled 'medical', 'security' and 'other' – identify a range of 'risk categories'. The 'other' column includes 'drugs/alcohol issues', 'suicide/self-harm' and 'vulnerability'. The PER also obliges the escort to keep a 'record of events' during transit. In addition to the PER the escort has a 'Prisoner Warning Notice' at their disposal in order to record any further relevant information in respect of the child's 'possible risk of self-harm or suicide'.

- Sixth, the *T1:V Form* is designed for the purposes of the 'reception' assessment (when children first arrive at penal custody) and it was first implemented in each of the 17 Prison Service Young Offender Institutions holding child prisoners in April 2001. 'National Standards' provide that 'all young people must be assessed for risk of self-harm and suicide on arrival' (Youth Justice Board, 2004b, para. 10.13) and, at the time the T1: V forms were first introduced, prison reception personnel were advised:

> 'The T1:V form is part of a set of ... documentation. Together these provide a system for ensuring that essential information about young people in custody is noted and communicated clearly... to provide appropriate care and supervision... Its purpose is to help staff undertaking the reception interview to assess the young person's vulnerability... and to make plans to minimise the risk of the young person harming themselves... while they are in custody. Vulnerability is susceptibility to significant physical or emotional harm and distress. Clear, accurate and shared assessments of the risk of harm will be successful in identifying ways to reduce the likelihood of such harm occurring'. (Youth Justice Board, 2001, p. 1)

- Seventh, the *Reception Health Screen*. In tandem with the reception interview and the completion of the T1:V documentation, children entering penal custody are also interviewed by a nurse from the Young Offender Institution's Health Care staff. The nurse is required to complete a further assessment form entitled the 'First Reception Health Screen'. The child prisoner is taken through a sequence of questions relating to their 'physical health', any 'drug/alcohol history' and their 'mental health' before being invited to offer any 'additional information'. The questions that feature within the mental health sequence are blunt and include: 'Have you ever deliberately harmed yourself?' and if so 'How and why?'; 'Have you ever attempted suicide?' and if so 'Method tried?'; 'Has any close relative or friend ever attempted suicide?'; 'Do you feel like hurting yourself at the moment?' and 'Are you feeling suicidal?'

Multiple methods of assessment have become an integral feature of penal process in respect of child prisoners. They are designed to minimise the likelihood of child death, harm and damage and, as such, they coexist with a range of child protection policies, practices and procedures.

Protection

Substantial effort has focussed upon developing child protection policies, practices and procedures and this effort was galvanised following an action for judicial review brought by the Howard League for Penal Reform in November 2002. Prior to this action, the statutory protections provided by the Children Act 1989 were taken as *not* applying to children in penal custody. As Valier (2004, p. 15) has observed, however, 'the League successfully challenged the legality of the Home Secretary's policy on statutory child protection duties towards children held in young offender institutions'. This book is not the place to engage with the detail of either the Howard League's case, or the judgement reached by Mr Justice Munby in the High Court (Munby, 2002). Suffice to note that since the judgement:

• The Association of Directors of Social Services, the Local Government Association and the Youth Justice Board for England and Wales, have made a series of recommendations in respect of the applicability of the Children Act 1989 to children in penal custody and the associated duties of statutory agencies, to ensure that robust child protection processes are in place (Association of Directors of Social Services, Local Government Association, Youth Justice Board for England and Wales 2003).
• Prison Service Order 4950 'Regimes for Under 18 year Olds', has been revised and now includes a detailed sequence of 'annexes' and 'appendices' setting out child protection law, guidance, policy, procedure, process and practice together with a range of pro-forma documents for the purposes of executing and recording child protection interventions in penal custody (Her Majesty's Prison Service, 2003).
• Her Majesty's Prison Service 'Juvenile Group' in partnership with the Youth Justice Board for England and Wales (2003) have undertaken a 'Child Protection and Safeguards Review'.
• Her Majesty's Prison Service 'Safer Custody Group' is piloting – in five prisons from January 2004 – new 'Assessment, Care in Custody and Teamwork' (ACCT) 'Care Plans', with a view to replacing the F2052SH forms and procedures that have been operational since 1992.
• The Department for Education and Skills (2004) has issued a Local Authority Circular entitled 'Safeguarding and promoting the welfare of children and young people in custody'. Amongst other things, the Circular advises Local Authorities, in areas where there is a Young Offender Institution or Secure Training Centre, to 'ensure that they have agreed local protocols with custodial establishments... in line with legislation, guidance and local procedures, including the local Area Child Protection Committee

(ACPC) child protection procedures' (*ibid*, p. 2.)
• The Youth Justice Board for England and Wales has issued a three-year 'Strategy for the Secure Estate for Juveniles' in which it states its determination to 'ensure that young offenders are cared for in custodial establishments where they are kept safe and healthy in decent conditions' (Youth Justice Board, 2004a, p.14).

'Safer custody' – A contradiction in terms?

'We were appointed to this strange job a year ago. As we celebrated, a young man was strangling to death... This kind of coincidence neatly typifies most of our subsequent experience as INQUEST workers. Whenever some small advance gave cause for satisfaction, a fresh wave of custodial deaths could be relied on to mar any sense of triumph'. (Leadbetter and Ward, cited in INQUEST, 2001, p.3)

'Reformers come and reformers go. State institutions carry on. Nothing in their history suggests that they can sustain reform, no matter what money, staff, and programs are pumped into them. The same crises that have plagued them for 150 years intrude today. Though the casts may change, the players go on producing failure'. (Miller, 1991, p.18)

In recent years, as noted above, considerable effort has been invested towards developing policies, practices and procedures aimed at minimising the risk of child death, harm and damage in penal custody. Yet the material impact of 'safer custody' initiatives requires critical analysis and contextualisation. On one level such reforms provide reassurance. On another, as Medlicott (2001, p. 219) has observed: 'many so-called policies, after all, exist more at the level of claim and representation on paper than in operational practice'. Despite, various child protection policies and procedures, for example, in practice progress is 'patchy' (Her Majesty's Chief Inspector of Prisons, 2005, p.56). It is indeed a bitter paradox, that the consolidation and development of the 'safer custody' imperative has been accompanied by record levels of self-inflicted death, harm and damage (Her Majesty's Chief Inspector of Prisons, 2004b). There are several reasons why this is so.

Tensions in policy and practice

The ostensible 'humanisation' of penal custody for children is, in some senses at least, intrinsically counter-productive. As Cohen (1985, p. 98) observed so perceptively twenty years ago: 'it is by making the system appear less harsh, that people are encouraged to use it more often'. Given that the Courts have been consistently presented with the message that the harmful excesses of penal custody are being 'designed-out' through a process of reform, therefore, and, moreover, that 'standards' have been 'pushed-up' to such an extent that detention can serve a 'constructive' purpose (Youth Justice Board, 2000b and 2004a), it is no surprise that they have tended to apply their custodial remand and sentencing powers with increasing regularity. Furthermore, this phenomenon is accentuated by New Labour's unrelenting determination to be seen to be 'tough on crime', as noted earlier. Penal expansion, and the problems that accompany it, inevitably follow.

The tensions between punitive policies and practices that ultimately serve to increase the use of penal custody for children on the one hand, and more benign responses that aim to take account of children's individual needs on the other, are apparent. Such tensions impose enormous pressures upon the 'juvenile secure estate'. The increasing rate of child imprisonment not only serves to diminish the latitude of the 'estate' to provide placement flexibility; it also circumscribes the time available for staff to provide individually-tailored assessment and intervention (Goldson, 2002b). Given that most 'placements' within the 'juvenile secure estate' are located within Young Offender Institutions, it follows that at any one time significant numbers of manifestly vulnerable children are inappropriately 'placed' in prisons. This compounds the pressure on staff to the point where sickness has reached record levels, currently higher than any other part of the public sector (Prison Reform Trust, 2004b). In turn, high levels of staff sickness have an adverse effect on morale and, more tangibly, it means that prison personnel have to cover the duties of absent colleagues, often working with children about whom they have limited (if any) personal knowledge. The 'vicious circle' effect is unavoidable, within which the care and protection of child prisoners are routinely neglected, sometimes with fatal consequences.

Information breakdown

Despite the introduction of the multiple and ostensibly 'joined-up' modes of assessment that we considered earlier, evidence suggests that in practice such processes 'haemorrhage' significant quantities of crucially relevant information. The Youth Justice Board has expressed concern about information breakdown and efforts have been made to address it. For example, in a circular to all YOT Managers, Local Authority Secure Unit Managers, YOI Governors and Secure Training Centre Managers in 2000, the Board reported that:

'It is still the case that young people are continuing to arrive at facilities with inadequate paperwork. Again this is particularly true of prison service placements. The relevant paperwork (Asset...post-court report) must be conveyed to the receiving unit with the young person, or by fax. We will be monitoring these matters and giving feedback to relevant YOTs'. (Youth Justice Board, 2000c, para. 8)

Despite the circular issued in 2000, together with the requirements of 'National Standards' discussed earlier, research evidence suggests that there had been little improvement by 2002 (Goldson, 2002b). Detailed interviews with prison personnel revealed that staff regularly have to work with exceptionally vulnerable children with little or no information in respect of their backgrounds, needs and risks (*ibid*, pp. 127-143).

Furthermore, in order to glean a quantitative representation of the extent of information breakdown, an audit of Post-Court Reports and Asset documentation was implemented in one YOI over a six month period (*ibid*, pp. 92-94). The audit related to every child prisoner remanded to the YOI. From the figures set-out in Table 5 the extent of information breakdown is apparent:

Table 5:	Child Remand Prisoners, Post-Court Reports (PCRs) and Asset Documentation Received in one YOI over 6 months						
	Month 1	Month 2	Month 3	Month 4	Month 5	Month 6	Totals
Child Remand Prisoners Received[1]	53	41	40	53	61	50	298
PCRs Received (% of total)	34 (64%)	25 (61%)	28 (70%)	38 (72%)	46 (75%)	32 (64%)	203 (68%)
ASSETs Received[2] (% of total)	14 (26%)	14 (34%)	15 (38%)	24 (45%)	24 (39%)	17 (34%)	108 (36%)
Both PCR and ASSET Received (% of total)	13 (26%)	9 (22%)	9 (22%)	16 (30%)	22 (36%)	13 (26%)	82 (28%)
Neither PCR nor ASSET Received (% of total)	15 (28%)	8 (20%)	6 (15%)	7 (13%)	10 (16%)	12 (24%)	58 (19%)

1. This relates to first remand and initial arrival at the YOI.
2. This relates to Bail ASSET and/or full ASSET.

- Only 203 PCRs were received in respect of 298 children (68 per cent of the total) or, to put it another way, 95 PCRs (32 per cent of the total) were 'lost' between the court and the YOI.
- A substantially worse rate of haemorrhage is evident in relation to Asset documentation. The YOI only received 108 Asset forms in respect of the 298 child remand prisoners (that is 36 per cent of the total). This represents a 64 per cent haemorrhage rate.
- Although, in accordance with National Standards, the YOI should receive a PCR *and* an Asset form in respect of *every* child remand prisoner, this occurred in only 28 per cent of cases during the audit period.
- With regard to 58 children (19 per cent of the total), the YOI received *neither* a PCR *nor* an Asset. This essentially means that YOI reception staff had absolutely no substantive information in respect of one in five child remand prisoners.

Given the importance attributed to assessment documentation within the context of 'safer custody', the extent of information breakdown is a significant concern.

In 2004 the Youth Justice Board (2004a; 2004b) introduced a new system, and issued guidance to YOTs, for communicating 'essential information for custodial facilities'. This requires YOTs to collate 'essential information' (including the Post-Court Report; Asset; Pre-Sentence Report; Placement Authorisation form and 'other forms', see above) and enter it into a distinctive 'yellow envelope' for transmission to custodial facilities. In particular, the guidance emphasises the importance of the Asset form and the Post-Court Report and it provides that both 'must' be completed 'in all cases' when children are sentenced and/or remanded to penal custody. This may, or may not succeed, where previously issued 'National Standards' and Youth Justice Board Circulars have seemingly failed, in reducing the extent of information breakdown. Youth Justice Board statistics (2005, p.90) provide mixed messages. They suggest that the extent of information breakdown has been curtailed and yet they also signal that, in 22 per cent of cases, Asset forms are not received by Young Offender Institutions at the point when children arrive. Irrespective of the effect of the new practices and procedures however, the problems associated with 'assessment' go further.

Flawed assessment

Despite the development of numerous assessment policies, practices and procedures directed at 'screening out' those children thought to be at greatest risk of death, harm and damage in penal custody, the reality is that the effectiveness of such responses continues to be severely limited. Towl and Crighton (2000, p. 91) have explained that 'risk assessment and risk management is concerned with uncertainty [and] as such, it is logically impossible for any risk assessment, however good, to predict an outcome with 100 per cent accuracy'. In other words, even the most thorough and expertly executed assessments cannot guarantee safety. It follows, therefore, that institutionally expedient, hasty and cursory 'assessments', of the type routinely applied to children in prisons (Goldson, 2002b), are flawed. It is of no surprise then, as the Department of Health (2004, Evidence 23) has observed that: 'the majority of deaths [in penal custody] occur in people who have not been recognised as being vulnerable to suicide at that time' (see also McHugh and Snow, 2000, p. 21).

Indeed, there is no single profile of the child who will self-harm or attempt suicide in penal custody. Some children who conform to stereotypical constructions of 'vulnerability' appear to 'cope' without incident, whilst others who might be expected to 'do their time' unproblematically experience serious difficulties. Individual reactions to emotional pain and environmental pressure differ and confound tidy prediction. While the process of refining and re-refining assessment techniques and technologies is understandable, therefore, it ultimately fails to provide effective safeguards against death, harm and damage. Any pretence otherwise is both misguided and misguiding.

Unsafe enclosures

The concept of 'safer custody' or the 'caring prison' (Prisons and Probation Ombudsman, 2004, Ev. 68) is, in essence, an oxymoron. There is little or no evidence to imply that the innumerable policies, practices and procedures designed to provide safe environments for children in penal custody have succeeded. The intrinsic tensions within policy and practice, systemic failings and information breakdown and the inevitable imperfections of assessment itself, combine to thwart even the prospect of securing safety, care and protection. More significantly, even when guidance is followed and standards are applied – when the system works as it should – penal custody remains, by definition, an unsafe enclosure for children. The evidence for such a proposition is found in the routine damage that continues to afflict children in prisons and other locked institutions and, at the extremes, the abiding presence of child death.

Case summaries: Joseph Scholes, Gareth Myatt and Adam Rickwood

Joseph Scholes: Died March 24 2002 aged 16 years

Joseph was born on February 20 1986 in Manchester. He had an unsettled childhood and became increasingly distressed through adolescence. Joseph's parents had divorced under difficult circumstances in 1997 culminating in 'a bitter custody battle' (INQUEST and Nacro, 2003, p. 2). Moreover, 'from the age of six he had allegedly suffered repeated and severe sexual abuse by a member of his father's family' (*ibid*, p.2).

Yvonne Scholes, Joseph's mother with whom he lived after the divorce, has described Joseph as always being young for his age. He was afraid of the dark and he would regularly seek reassurance and comfort during the night. At the age of 15 years Joseph was still climbing trees and building dens. Yvonne also recalls noticing relatively minor injuries on her son's body. Joseph initially accounted for such grazes, lumps and bruises by explaining that they were caused during play. However, as the injuries worsened Yvonne 'came to the unpleasant realisation that her son was deliberately harming himself' (Bennett, 2004, p. 2). Moreover, as he became older Joseph's distress expressed itself more vividly through a 'horrific catalogue of self-abuse' (*ibid*, p.2). The strain of managing Joseph's increasingly challenging and self-harming behaviour eventually became too much for Yvonne to bear. With three other children to look after she reluctantly arranged, in October 2001, for Joseph to live with his father.

Joseph's stay with his father was brief. After only six weeks he was received into the care of the Local Authority and placed in a Children's Home where the Residential Social Work staff described him as well-mannered and polite. On December 6 2001 however, just a week after his arrival, Joseph went out with four other children from the Home, two boys and two girls. The evening started innocently enough but became problematic. After a spontaneous bout of drinking strong alcohol the children came across another group of youngsters and demanded their money and mobile telephones. Joseph, along with his companions, was subsequently arrested. Such behaviour was out of character. Joseph was no seasoned young offender and yet in the eyes of the law he was now facing the serious charge of street robbery.

As Joseph's court appearance drew closer he became increasingly anxious and agitated. On one occasion, in the privacy of his bedroom at the Children's Home, he took a knife to his face and inflicted more than 30 slash wounds, the deepest of which cut to the bone on the bridge of his nose. On February 26, 2001 Joseph entered a guilty plea to Manchester Crown Court. It was accepted that although present, and by definition culpable, Joseph's role in the offence was largely peripheral. The judge requested reports and adjourned the case until March 15, 2001.

When Joseph re-appeared in court for sentence the Prosecutor explicitly stated to the Judge that 'Joseph Scholes offered no physical violence to any person on December 6, 2001' (cited in Bennett, 2004, p. 3). The Judge also had the benefit of reports from Residential Social Workers, the Youth

Offending Service and a Consultant Child and Adolescent Psychiatrist, all of which identified Joseph's manifest vulnerability, 'his experience of sexual abuse and history of suicidal and self-harming behaviour' (House of Lords House of Commons Joint Committee on Human Rights, 2004b, para. 74) and the likely risks if he were to be sent to prison custody. The Judge, cognisant of such expert testimony, stated in open court that he wanted Joseph's history 'most expressly drawn to the attention of the authorities' (INQUEST and Nacro, 2003, p. 2). He also claimed, however, that: 'it is an unhappy fact that these serious offences of street robbery are against a background of anxiety and fear the length and breadth of this country and only in the last couple of weeks, the Lord Chief Justice has said what has always been the policy in my court, that is that people... committing street robberies, receive immediate custodial sentences' (cited in Bennett, p.4). The Judge sentenced Joseph to two years, fully exploiting the maximum and most severe sentencing powers available to him in the circumstances.

Although the Judge imposed the sentence of penal custody, the Youth Justice Board for England and Wales might have elected to place Joseph in a non-prison sector secure setting. However, no alternative placement was available. Accordingly, on March 15, 2001 Joseph was taken to Her Majesty's Young Offender Institution Stoke Heath, near Market Drayton, Shropshire. Upon arrival at Stoke Heath Joseph was initially placed in a more-or-less bare cell under the gaze of a surveillance camera and intense levels of observation. He was dressed in a heavy canvas garment with stiff velcro fastenings under which he was naked. Such conditions are described by the Prison Service as 'safe'. A national childcare expert, called to give evidence at Joseph's inquest, described them as 'dehumanising'. Joseph repeatedly told prison officers and other professional personnel that he would take his own life if he was moved to 'normal location' within the prison. His history of sexual abuse had left him with enduring fears. Yet the prison officers implemented an incremental transitionary process that would ultimately lead to his transfer on to the main prison wing. Within days of his arrival at Stoke Heath this process commenced and Joseph was moved to another cell within the Health Care Centre within which he was less intensively observed. The move was to prove fatal.

On the afternoon of Sunday March 24, 2001, on the ninth day of his two year sentence, Joseph placed a noose, made from a bed-sheet, around his neck and hung himself from the bars of his cell. His body was discovered by a maintenance worker who had been called to the Health Care Centre to attend to blocked toilets. Joseph left a message: 'I love you mum and dad. I'm sorry I just can't cope. Don't be sad. It's no one's fault. I just can't go on. None of it was any of your fault, sorry. Love you and family, Joe'. His very final words are haunting: 'I tried telling them and they just don't fucking listen'. Joseph died alone in a dirty and barren prison cell. He was just 16 years old.

Gareth Myatt: Died April 19 2004 aged 15 years

Gareth lived in Stoke-on-Trent, Staffordshire where he had been in the care of the Local Authority since 1997 (Travis, 2004). On 16 April, 2004 he was made the subject of a twelve month Detention and Training Order for offences of assault and theft. Gareth was sent to Rainsbrook Secure Training Centre in Northamptonshire. Rainsbrook opened in July 1999 as one of three privately owned children's jails in England. It is operated by Rebound EDC, a subsidiary of the security company Group 4.

Gareth was a very slight boy; little more than five feet tall and weighing less than eight stone. On the evening of April 19, however, just three days into his sentence, three members of Rainsbrook staff (two men and a woman) felt it necessary to physically 'restrain' him. Gareth was subjected to a 'seated double embrace' 'restraint' technique during which he lost consciousness. A Duty Nurse failed in attempts to resuscitate him and an ambulance was called at 9.42p.m. Gareth was taken to Walsgrave Hospital in Coventry where he was pronounced dead at 10.25p.m. A postmortem examination was carried out the day after his death but the results were inconclusive

Gareth's death has given rise to three separate inquiries by state agencies. First, Detective Chief Inspector Charles Moffat from Northamptonshire Police reported that the initial investigation and the views of independent experts 'had raised potential concerns about the medical consequences of the restraint used on Gareth the night that he died'. The use of the 'seated double embrace' 'restraint' technique has since been suspended following advice from the Police (Bateman, 2004b). Second, Stoke-on-Trent Area Child Protection Committee is conducting a 'Part 8' inquiry in accordance with the provisions of official guidance (Department of Health *et al*, 1999). Third, the Youth Justice Board for England and Wales commissioned David Gilroy, a former Deputy Chief Inspector of Social Services, to lead an investigation. Furthermore, the Howard League for Penal Reform commissioned Lord Alex Carlile QC, together with an Advisory Panel of experts, to undertake an independent inquiry into the general application of 'restraint' techniques in penal facilities for children. This follows the publication of evidence, derived from responses to Parliamentary Questions, showing that physical 'restraint' was applied on '11,953 occasions in the three Secure Training Centres in England since 1999, even though the institutions hold on average just 190 children at any one time' (Press Association, 2004).

At the time of writing, none of the findings from either of the three state agency inquiries, or the independent inquiry, have been published or have otherwise entered the public domain. In the meantime, however, INQUEST has made two important observations. First, the widespread application of physical interventions with children in penal custody in general, and the death of Gareth in particular: 'begs the question about how... potentially lethal methods of restraint were being used against children and what medical advice was taken before such methods were introduced' (INQUEST, 2004c, p.5). Second, equally serious questions are raised by the fact that Gareth was a black child. Indeed, for many years INQUEST and other agencies have expressed concerns about the disproportionate use of 'restraint' techniques and the over-representation of black people with regard to 'restraint' related deaths (*ibid*).

Gareth died on the very same day that the inquest opened in Shrewsbury Coroner's Court into the death of 16 year old Joseph Scholes. At the time of his death 15 years old Gareth Myatt was the youngest person in living memory to die not by their own hand in penal custody in the UK (*ibid*).

Adam Rickwood: Died August 9 2004 aged 14 years

Adam was a lively popular child who lived in Burnley, Lancashire with his mother, step-father and three sisters. He also had his share of troubles. Whilst growing-up he was devoted to his grandparents, yet three of them died within a period of 18 months, the first when he was just 11 years old. This had a negative effect on Adam at precisely the time that he was making the transition between primary and secondary school. He struggled and his difficulties ultimately led to him being excluded from school. He also had a history of self harming behaviour and wrist-cutting and he had been admitted to Burnley General Hospital on at least one occasion, having taken an overdose of tablets. Adam's mother made concerted efforts to secure professional help for her son with limited success. His surviving grandmother explained that: 'my daughter battered her head off every wall she could find to get help for her son' (cited in Branigan, 2004).

Adam also had a number of minor scrapes with the law, mostly limited to Police warnings for riding old motor cycles over open ground near to his home. However, on one occasion Adam clashed with a man in his 20s, resulting in him facing serious charges for wounding. On appearing in court he was bailed on condition that he wore an electronic monitoring tag. Adam complied with this condition until, according to his grandmother, he removed it 'as a prank' (cited in Branigan, 2004). 'Prank' it might have been to Adam, but the Court took a different view. For breaching conditions of bail, Adam was sent to

Hassockfield Secure Training Centre near Consett, County Durham, some 150 miles away from his family in Burnley. Hassockfield is a privately managed children's jail owned by the Premier Custodial Group and operated through its Medomsley Training Services subsidiary (Morris, 2004).

Despite the 300 mile round trip, Adam's family made regular visits to see him during which they became increasingly concerned with his burgeoning emotional fragility. His mother has reported that she had asked for him to be closely monitored. On August 9, 2004 Adam was due to re-appear in court in order to attend a further bail application. He never made it. In the early hours of that morning Adam was found hanging in his cell. In the words of his grandmother he was 'a little boy trying to live in a big man's world'. She continued: 'there's other little boys and girls in there [Hassockfield]. It's horrendous. They're only babies' (cited in Branigan, 2004). Adam Rickwood became a particularly sad statistic: the 27th 'little boy' to lose his life in penal custody in England and Wales since 1990 and the youngest penal fatality in modern times (INQUEST, 2004c).

As noted above, from the time of Philip Knight's death at HMP Swansea in July 1990, to the time of Gareth Price's death at HMYOI Lancaster Farms in January 2005, substantial effort has been invested in attempts to establish 'safer custody' and minimise the prospect of death, harm and damage. Despite all of this, however, 28 children have died and literally thousands more have been damaged. Some ten years ago, Coles and Ward (1994, p. 142) expressed their 'exasperation' at the recurrence of deaths in penal custody. At best 'there are many deaths where everyone concerned seems to have acted quite reasonably within the constraints of the system'. At worse 'inquest after inquest, year after year, reveals the same administrative and medical blunders, the same failures of communication, the same almost willful blindness to prisoners' distress' (*ibid*, p.142). It is not our intention here to make judgements in respect of individual cases and/or to apportion blame, rather to note that despite all of the policy, practice and procedural reform, little appears to have changed materially for the better. When all is said and done, 28 children are dead and the core lessons are yet to be learned.

Chapter 4
Post-Death Investigations and Inquests

'It is perhaps one of the most obvious human paradoxes that death is an integral part of life. In the normal course of events the routine death of a member of the family or a friend is a deep, private grief... However there are deaths that are far from routine and that invoke quite different responses... public disputation... and raise wider questions about the culpability of state officials... In other words they become matters of public concern'. (Ryan, 1996, p. 1)

'[T]he state must be presumed to have failed if a person dies in its custody. Therefore there needs to be a thorough investigation of any death, because any fault in the system for protecting the right to life could very well lead to another loss of life. The state has [also] failed ... if it does not investigate the death properly'. (Liberty, 2003, p.1)

'[T]he fundamental rights of the deceased and their families are not properly respected by the inquest system in Britain. Moreover, the current system enables institutions of the state to be insufficiently scrutinised when people die as a consequence of acts and omissions by its agents. We believe that the provision of an inadequate inquiry in such circumstances damages the bereaved and undermines the quality and legitimacy of the public authorities whose conduct has gone without scrutiny. This adversely affects us all'. (Thomas, Friedman and Christian, 2002, p. vii)

'Any new system [of investigations and inquests] needs to operate within a framework that ensures openness, accountability, compatibility with the Human Rights Act and sensitivity to bereaved people and the public. To establish such a framework there needs to be clear national protocols for all aspects of post-death investigation... Above all it needs to be a system that balances the needs of the State with those of bereaved people and ensures that all participants have an equality of resources and information. Whilst the process will be painful for bereaved people it will be more bearable if it is seen to have legitimacy and meaningful outcomes'. (Coles and Shaw, 2002, p. 4)

Introduction

Whilst child deaths in penal custody are not uncommon, neither are they 'routine'. Quite properly, therefore, such deaths are 'matters of public concern'. In cases where death is self-inflicted and the police are satisfied that there are no grounds for prosecution, at least two separate but related processes are conventionally activated.[1] First, an *investigation* into the specific circumstances surrounding the child's death in the penal institution will take place. Second, the Coroner's Court, covering the geographical area within which the body is finally located, will be notified and the Coroner will preside over an *inquest*. In more recent cases, including the deaths of Joseph Scholes and Adam Rickwood, additional investigative processes have also been applied involving 'Serious Incident Reviews', as developed by the Youth Justice Board for England and Wales, and 'Part 8 Reviews', initially provided by the Department of Health, Home Office and Department for Education and Employment guidance (1999). For the purposes here, however, we are primarily concerned with institutionally focused investigations and coroner's inquests.

On face value and taken together, investigations and inquests might appear to provide for comprehensive scrutiny in order that both the specific and more general circumstances of child deaths in penal custody may be fully examined. The investigatory and inquest apparatus relating to child deaths in penal custody, deaths in state institutions more generally (including adult prisons, police stations, psychiatric hospitals and other secure facilities), and deaths following 'disasters' that imply corporate liability are, however, surrounded by controversy. (See for example: Scraton and Chadwick, 1986 and 1987b; Scraton, Jemphrey and Coleman, 1995; Ryan, 1996; Beckett, 1999; Scraton, 1999; Coles and Shaw, 2002; Thomas *et al* 2002; Liberty, 2003; House of Lords House of Commons Joint Committee on Human Rights, 2004a and 2004b). This chapter, whilst striking some resonance with the broader and more general context, will serve primarily to analyse investigations and inquests as they relate to child deaths in penal custody.

---

1. At the time of writing Gareth Myatt's death remains open to police investigation.

In the same way that the 'safer custody' agenda has ushered in numerous reforms, similar reforming initiatives have focussed upon investigations and inquests. In other words, post-death processes are dynamic as distinct from static and, from the time of Philip Knight's death in July 1990 to the time of Gareth Price's death in January 2005, reforms have modified policy and practice. Furthermore, reforms are ongoing and at the time of writing further changes are imminent. Accordingly, in analysing post-death investigation and inquest systems we will engage critically with past, present and prospective policy and practice. Before turning to this however, attention will first focus upon the processes that are activated when representatives from state agencies are required to notify the child's next of kin following a death in penal custody.

Notifying the bereaved: 'your child is dead'

'[I]t is a fundamental requirement of the ... duty of care to handle the aftermath of a death with professionalism and sensitivity...'. (Snow and McHugh, 2000, p. 135)

'The way families are informed of a death and the treatment they receive from officialdom at this stage can crucially set the tone for the way they are able to interact with the whole process'. (Coles and Shaw, 2002, p.22)

'A death in custody, once it has occurred, requires respect for the rights of the family of the person who has died. During this inquiry we met family and relatives of people who had died in custody... Several of the families had been informed of a death in ways that were highly insensitive, and several had been given insufficient information about what had happened, or had been obstructed in their attempts to obtain information. In a number of cases we were told of, parents were informed of the death of a son by telephone... We were concerned... that in the immediate aftermath of a death, families are not always treated with the respect and consideration that they deserve'. (House of Lords House of Commons Joint Committee on Human Rights, 2004b, paras. 286-7)

To be informed that a child has died in penal custody is devastating for their immediate family. The manner in which families are notified of a death is a matter of crucial importance therefore, not only with regard to human decency and respect for the bereaved, but also in relation to the family's capacity to participate in the processes of investigation and inquest. The experiences of bereaved families in receiving notification of a child's death in penal custody are, by definition, individualised and family-specific and there is little by way of collated qualitative or quantitative data with which to gauge their collective experience. Direct practice experience, together with the research literature that is available (Coles and Shaw, 2002 and forthcoming, 2005; Davis, *et al*, 2002) however, paints an inconsistent, although primarily problematic, picture. Whilst it is true that a minority of families report receiving helpful and compassionate responses, for the majority the aftermath of their child's death is typically characterised at best by blundering inefficiency and, at worst, by insensitivity and a callous disregard to their grief. At the extremes families report feeling doubly victimised, even criminalised: 'they have suffered a death and because of its nature and the circumstances in which the death has occurred they are treated as though they are criminals' (Coles and Shaw, forthcoming, 2005).

Beckett (1999) interviewed families who reported the negative effects of receiving detailed but inaccurate accounts of deaths, whilst Coles and Shaw (2002, p. 52) have explained that: 'a lack of accurate information given at the time of being informed of the death has led... to further distress and suspicion about the whole process'. The most illuminating insights into the pain and distress induced by inept and/or insensitive notification and compounded by subsequent system neglect – experiences that are not uncommon for bereaved families – are best expressed by the families themselves. Yvonne Scholes for example, the mother of Joseph Scholes whose case was discussed in Chapter 3, has explained:

> 'I was contacted between three and four hours after my son died although the Home Office press office knew before me. A police officer came to my house and asked me if I was alone. I don't think he even told me that Joseph had died, I just screamed "He's dead, he's dead", ran inside, threw myself on the floor and kept having to run to the bathroom to vomit. I was utterly shocked... I found it inconceivable that Joseph had died while on the health care wing. Next day, the prison offered to send a chaplain but we declined. After that we were given INQUEST's number then left alone and had no further support from the prison or social services and little help from the police. I had difficulty walking, let alone driving and I had a disabled child to care for. Prison staff are offered support in these circumstances but families are totally disregarded'. (Cited in Jerrom, 2004, p.30)

Yvonne Scholes' experience is not an aberration. INQUEST has consistently referred to system 'failure' (see for example Coles and Shaw, 2002). Furthermore, a recent analysis of such failure led the House of Lords House of Commons Joint Committee on Human Rights to recommend that:

'All institutions of detention should develop and implement procedures to inform family members of a death promptly and sensitively, to provide them with appropriate support, advise them on how the post-mortem investigation will proceed, and to provide them, promptly, with information on the circumstances of the death... Staff members should be trained in effective liaison with families in these circumstances... Wherever possible, staff should visit the family to inform them in person of the death'. (House of Lords House of Commons Joint Committee on Human Rights, 2004b, para. 287)

Such a recommendation, alongside the prospect of improving investigation and inquest processes, is clearly welcome.

Investigations

'Since April 1998 all deaths in custody have been investigated by the Prison Service. Investigations are carried out by senior governors. Although "independent" of the prison concerned, investigating officers are usually from the same area and our investigations could not be regarded as other than internal. Investigating Officers act on behalf of the Commissioning Authority (CA), the area manager or equivalent, responsible for the establishment in which the death occurred, to whom they are accountable. The CAs are in turn accountable to the Director General and his Deputy. Currently therefore both the commissioning of investigations and "ownership" of reports rest with the operational line of the Prison Service'. (Her Majesty's Prison Service, 2004, Ev. 31).

'The investigations following prison deaths... are characterised by... a lack of independence'. (Liberty, 2003, p.26)

'I decry those who fail to acknowledge the significant changes for the better that have occurred'. (Prisons and Probation Ombudsman for England and Wales, 2004, Ev. 68)

In 1998, Her Majesty's Prison Service issued revised guidance and instructions on procedures to be followed after a death in custody (Prison Service Order 2710). The Prison Service Order (PSO) set out the key stages of the investigatory process including: immediate action on discovery of a body; reporting requirements; contact with the Prison Service's press office and media; support for staff and prisoners; follow-up support for the family involved; preparation for an internal investigation; contact with the coroner and arrangements for the inquest; funeral arrangements and disclosure of information to the family and their legal representatives (if any). Led by a senior prison governor from outside the institution within which the death occurred, the principal official purpose of such investigations was to examine the degree of compliance with policy and procedures and to consider whether there are any lessons to be learned that might improve practice and inform future policy development. Ostensibly, all of this appears to make good sense.

The PSO however, differentiated between 'mandatory action' and 'recommended good practice' and, as Snow and McHugh (2000, p. 153) observed: 'this distinction sometimes appears puzzling to those outside the Prison Service where the concept of discretion may seem at odds with the nature of the task in hand'. At the time of writing, a revised Prison Service Order 2710 ('Follow up to deaths in custody') has been drafted but publication has not yet been authorised and no implementation date has been fixed (INQUEST, 2005b). It is not possible to determine the impact, if any, that the new PSO might have in terms of limiting discretion therefore, but it is understood that the distinction between 'mandatory actions' or 'mandatory requirements' and good practice 'guidance' will remain. The question of discretionary leeway is not the only issue at stake, however. At least two other aspects of the investigatory process have attracted critical attention in recent years, each serving to initiate, at least in part, statutory reform.

First, there is the question of *disclosure of information*. Until April 1999, the policy of the Prison Service was to treat the reports of investigations into deaths in custody as confidential documents and, as such, they were not available for routine disclosure. Such secretive practice attracted widespread criticism, not least from bereaved families, their legal representatives (where applicable), organisations such as INQUEST and, ultimately, the Parliamentary Commission for Administration (1999) – following its inquiries into several complaints arising from deaths in penal custody. Such critical attention prompted a reform of policy and, so it is claimed, has marked a change of direction since April 1999: 'towards greater openness by allowing disclosure of the investigation report, *subject to the views of the coroner* and, *with some restrictions on security-sensitive or personal information,* prior to the inquest *to those whom the coroner identifies as properly interested parties*' (Snow and McHugh, 2000, p. 154, emphases added). Furthermore, in 2004 the Prisons and Probation Ombudsman assumed responsibility for post-death investigations (see below) and, in March 2005, new 'guidance on disclosure' was issued (Prisons and Probation Ombudsman for England and Wales, 2005).

The guidance (*ibid*, sub-section 1) expresses a 'commitment to full, fair, open and transparent investigations', adding that 'the question of *what information* should be disclosed to *whom* and *when* has to be set against the background of these fundamental principles' (emphases added). The guidance further states: 'the presumption is that disclosure should occur as fully and as early as [the Ombudsman's] powers and the law allows'. Despite such progress however, 'exemptions to disclosure' (*ibid*, sub-section 4) continue to apply and no *statutory* time limits have been specified in order to guarantee the early release of relevant documentation to families and their representatives (if any) (see below).

Second, there is the question of *independence*. It is perhaps inevitable that a process that retains substantial discretionary capacity and, up until 2004, ultimately relied upon the Prison Service to investigate itself, was unlikely to instil public confidence. Accordingly: 'in its 2002 White Paper, *Justice for All*, the Government said that it was considering whether to extend the remit of the Prisons and Probation Ombudsman's Office to include the investigation of self-inflicted deaths in custody' (Prisons and Probation Ombudsman for England and Wales, 2004, Ev. 67). Furthermore, in 2004 the Home Secretary requested that the Prisons and Probation Ombudsman investigate the death of a woman prisoner in HMP Styal making this: 'the first time that the investigation of a death in a British prison has been independently conducted' (*ibid*, Ev. 68). Since that time, as noted above, the Ombudsman has assumed responsibility for investigating all self-inflicted deaths in penal custody.[2]

If the PSO guidance that frames investigations into (child) deaths in penal custody implies that such processes are straightforward affairs however, the reality is otherwise. Moreover, if recent reforms with regard to 'disclosure of information' and 'independence' suggest that the principal sites of contestation and controversy have been 'designed-out', then the experiences of bereaved families and those who work most closely with them, articulate a quite different account. We shall return to these issues later in the chapter, but first we turn to a review of Coroner's inquests themselves.

Inquests

> 'Within our jurisprudence, the coroner's court is a fossil-like entity. It bears the layers of almost every era of legal history...'. (Liberty, 2003, p.11)

---

2. This responsibility extends to child deaths in Secure Training Centres in addition to those in Prison Service custody.

'In answering the question "how" the deceased died, the inquest is not a forum *where all the facts* surrounding the death are explored, and neither is the coroner bound to consider the *circumstances* in which a death took place'. (Thomas, Friedman and Christian, 2002, p. 6, emphases added)

'The narrow focus... puts artificial and invidious limits on the scope and style of conduct of the Coroner's inquiry, which often exclude from the inquest the issues of greatest concern to the family. The inquest is usually the only investigation of death to which a family has access. Importantly, for the public interest and democratic accountability, it is the only public forum in which contentious deaths will be subject to scrutiny. Inquests are too often at risk... of being opportunities for official and sanitised versions of deaths to be given judicial approval – rather than being an opportunity for the family to contest the evidence presented, to discover the truth and full circumstances surrounding the death of their loved one'. (Coles and Shaw, 2002, p.5)

The Coroner's Court was statutorily established by the Articles of Eyre in 1194 and since that time it has passed through various socio-legal metamorphoses. Today, the coroner's court is the forum within which inquests are heard and, although it remains shrouded in a certain mystery, its principal functions are quite narrowly defined. Inquests are governed by the Coroners Act (CA) 1988 and the Coroners Rules (CR) 1984.

Section 8 of the CA 1988 provides that there is a statutory duty to hold an inquest where there is 'reasonable cause to suspect' any death in prison, and/or any 'violent or unnatural death; or sudden death of which the cause is unknown'. Section 8 also requires that any inquest into the death of a person in *prison* must always be held before a jury and, Rule 17 of the CR 1984, stipulates that such inquests must also be held in public.[3] Furthermore, CA 1988 (s. 11) and CR 1984 (r. 36) provide that proceedings and evidence at an inquest should be directed exclusively towards addressing four key questions: who the deceased was?; *where* the deceased came by their death?; *when* the deceased came by their death? and *how* the deceased came by their death?

More significantly perhaps, inquests are statutorily defined as *inquisitorial* 'fact finding' exercises as distinct from *adversarial* processes designed to apportion responsibility, liability, blame and/or guilt. Furthermore, the narrow

---

3. It is not yet clear whether or not this will also apply to inquests following child deaths in Secure Training Centres.

focus and restricted nature of inquests is underlined by Rules 36 and 42 of CR 1984 that state:

> 'Neither the coroner nor the jury shall express any opinion on any other matters'. (R. 36(2))

and

> 'No verdict shall be framed in such a way as to appear to determine any question of -
> (a) criminal liability on the part of the named person, or
> (b) civil liability'. (R. 42)

Thus there are no 'parties', formal 'charges' or 'pleadings' at inquests and no 'cross-examination' of witnesses. Rather, in the case of a child's death in penal custody, the coroner is primarily tasked with ensuring that a 'factual' account of the death is presented and that relevant witnesses are called to give evidence – witnesses who may be questioned by 'properly interested persons' – for the purposes of determining *where*, *when* and *how* the child died.

Not unlike investigations, inquests have attracted a great deal of critical attention. Indeed, leading legal commentators have noted that:

> 'The purpose and function of an inquest are matters that have been the subject of considerable legal and political debate. The boundaries of what an inquest is capable of achieving, even in legal terms, are tremendously variable. In the first instance it can be said without any doubt that an inquest is not a trial... The question arises, if the inquest is not a trial, is the hearing a tribunal or a court? In *R v Surrey ex p Campbell* the tensions and apparent resolution of the various purposes and functions of the coroner's court were referred to... in this way: "... its function is to investigate but not to reach a final decision such as a judgement order or a verdict of guilt"'. (Thomas *et al*, 2002, p.162)

It might be argued, therefore, that the narrow confines within which inquests operate are, in effect, prohibitive: they can serve to conceal more than they reveal in respect of the broader circumstances within which child deaths in penal custody are located. Again, not unlike investigations, such critiques, at least in part, have prompted a series of reforms.

In July 2001 the Home Office established a 'Fundamental Review of Death Certification and Coroner Services' and the review team reported in June 2003;

offering 123 recommendations covering organisation, resources, procedure verdicts and family rights (Home Office, 2003c). Subsequently, commentators have noted that: 'it is widely anticipated that there will be changes to substantive and procedural inquest law, as well as to the organisation and resourcing of the system' (Doughty Street Chambers, 2004, Ev. 87). Alongside actual reforms and proposals for further reforms, that might be conceived as responses to the critical attention that Coroners Courts and the system of inquests have attracted, the European Convention on Human Rights and the Human Rights Act 1998, together with related case law, have also contributed significantly to the drive for change.

The European Convention on Human Rights and the Human Rights Act 1998: towards better practice?

'It now appears that the incorporation of the European Convention on Human Rights (ECHR) by the Human Rights Act (HRA) 1998 may have a fundamental impact on the inquest system'. (Howe, 2004, Ev. 122)

'The most significant recent development in coronial law has to be the implementation of the Human Rights Act and the direct incorporation of Article 2 [of the European Convention on Human Rights] into domestic law'. (INQUEST, 2003b, p.17)

'The Inquest is the main forum in which the Article 2 investigatory duty is discharged in the majority of deaths in custody cases in England, Wales and Northern Ireland'. (House of Lords House of Commons Joint Committee on Human Rights, 2004b, para. 288)

Article 2 of the European Convention on Human Rights (ECHR), the 'Right to Life', is taken to be the most fundamental of human rights. Article 2(1) provides that a person's right to life 'shall be protected by law' and the state is required to take steps to safeguard the lives of those within its jurisdiction. More specifically, this right has also been identified as extending to taking positive steps to prevent self-inflicted deaths in penal custody. Owen and Friedman (2002, p.1), for example, observe that: 'a series of important decisions... in Strasbourg and subsequently in the domestic courts significantly illuminated the nature of the State's obligation to take active steps to prevent suicide and self-harm in custody'. Furthermore (Liberty, 2004, Ev. 103) has noted:

'The obligation to take positive steps to protect life also requires some form of *investigation* where death has occurred in a way that engages Article 2 or 3 of the Convention. The lack of an *effective investigation* will in itself constitute a *violation* of Article 2. This extends beyond deaths that occur as a result of the actions of those who work for the state to self-inflicted deaths in prison'. (Emphases added)

The procedural obligation that arises under Article 2, to conduct an 'effective investigation', has obvious implications for investigations and inquests. Furthermore, as noted, important developments in case-law have established a range of criteria for an 'effective investigation' (also see later). By building upon those criteria, remaining cognisant of relevant statutes and the critical attention that investigations and inquests have attracted, and by applying principles of 'best practice', it is reasonable to conclude that investigations and inquests in respect of child deaths in penal custody should be underpinned by and/or facilitate the application of five core principles:

- First, *state initiative and independence*. Investigations and inquests should be proactively instigated by state authorities as distinct from awaiting complaints, allegations and/or proceedings from bereaved families. Such processes should be managed and implemented in a way that is entirely independent from any agencies and/or personnel who might be implicated in the death of the child. The same processes should be capable of demonstrating such independence.
- Second, *effectiveness and disclosure*. Investigations and inquests, if they are to be effective, must be appropriately resourced and legally empowered to determine questions of culpability and liability and, where appropriate, to identify those responsible for a child's death. The full and unobstructed disclosure of relevant evidence and information should be available to all 'parties' (perhaps especially the child's family) in order to facilitate the search for 'truth' and, if necessary, lay the foundations for prosecution.
- Third, *promptness and reasonable expedition*. Investigations and inquests should commence without undue delay after a child's death and should progress as expeditiously as possible, without compromising the depth and thoroughness of the investigatory process.
- Fourth, *transparency and integrity*. If investigations and inquests are to earn the respect and confidence of the public, and particularly the bereaved, they should be open to sufficient public scrutiny to ensure accountability. Consistent with the questions of independence and disclosure, 'closed'

practices and cultures of organisational/institutional secrecy should be erased.

- Fifth, *family participation*. Investigations and inquests should allow for the fullest participation of the bereaved to the extent necessary to satisfy and protect their legitimate interests.

Such principles offer a 'benchmarking' framework within which past and present policy and practice can be critically analysed.

Analysing investigations

State initiative and independence

'All the investigators into deaths in prison are currently employees of the Prison Service. These investigators have often been unable to establish a relationship with families who are very often not confident in the way a death is being investigated because it is not seen as independent of the prison service... A clear need for independent investigators is required'. (INQUEST, 2003b, p.14)

'When a death occurs in custody, the independence of an investigation is crucial'. (Howe, 2004, Ev. 123)

'All future deaths... will be investigated by the Prisons and Probation Ombudsman from 1 April 2004... Welcoming the announcement of his office's extended role... the Prisons and Probation Ombudsman, said: "In taking on the daunting responsibility of investigating deaths in custody, I have three main aims. First, to enhance public confidence when someone has died while in the hands of the state. Second, to involve and to provide answers for bereaved relatives. Third, to contribute to the efforts of the Prison Service and others to reduce the numbers of self-inflicted and other avoidable deaths"'. (Home Office, 2004b, p.1)

As noted earlier, it has been traditional practice for the Prison Service to investigate itself in cases of child deaths (and all other self-inflicted deaths) in penal custody and, for many years, the absence of independent investigation has been a source of fundamental concern. Indeed, this practice applied to each of the cases from Philip Knight in July 1990 to Ian Powell in October 2002; 25 of the 28 child deaths considered in this book. Since 1 April 2004, however, the Prisons and Probation Ombudsman has been responsible for conducting 'independent' inquiries into *all* deaths in prisons. The transfer of the investigatory function from the Prison Service to the Ombudsman was designed to provide 'independent investigation' as a duty of compliance with the European Convention on Human Rights and the Human Rights Act 1998. Whilst such reform may be taken to signal progress however, it falls short of establishing a truly independent investigatory system on at least three levels.

First, the Ombudsman's investigatory function is, at the time of writing, being exercised on a non-statutory basis and the office has no power to *compel* the production of evidence. In May 2003 the Home Office (2003d, para. 1, emphases added) stated that 'the government feels that such a critical appointment should have a clear *statutory basis* and intends to legislate to achieve this *as soon as possible*'. To-date, however, no such legislation has been forthcoming. Indeed, in December 2004, more than eighteen months after the Home Office issued this statement the House of Lords House of Commons Joint Committee on Human Rights reported:

> 'In both written and oral evidence we were *overwhelmingly* met with concern that the Prisons and Probation Ombudsman was still *not on a statutory footing*, and that this would *undermine the independence*, and perception of independence, of inquiries into deaths in custody'. (House of Lords House of Commons Joint Committee on Human Rights, 2004b, para. 331, emphasis added)

Furthermore, with regard to the question of compliance with the European Convention on Human Rights and the Human Rights Act 1998, the Prisons and Probation Ombudsman has stated:

> 'The judgement as to whether or not an investigation of mine has met Article 2 or not is not a matter for me but for the courts, but my own feeling is that in itself it *manifestly does not*'. (Cited in House of Lords House of Commons Joint Committee on Human Rights, 2004b, para. 331, emphasis added)

Second, Liberty observed that:

> 'It is vital that sufficient resources are made available to the PPO [Prisons and Probation Ombudsman]... It is important not to underestimate the resources needed for a proper, thorough and effective investigation which complies with the requirements of Article 2'. (Liberty, 2004, Ev. 104)

There is no evidence to suggest that the necessary resources have been made available to the Prisons and Probation Ombudsman, however.

Third, and most importantly, the very independence of the Prisons and Probation Ombudsman is itself open to question:

> 'At the moment, the post of the... Ombudsman is *too strongly connected with the Home Office*. Liberty and INQUEST believe that the *lack of genuine demonstrable independence* from the Prison Service leaves the Ombudsman's role vulnerable to criticism that it is not a truly independent body. Many of his staff are Home Office employees on secondment which again, without radical change, would undermine confidence'. (Liberty, 2003, p. 65, emphases added)

Effectiveness and disclosure

> '[An] issue which cannot be separated from either the lack of independence of initial investigations of deaths in custody or the *ineffectiveness*... [is] the *lack of disclosure* to... families of those who have died. Despite recent pledges towards a more open system, any internal investigation statements taken from witnesses are the property of the Prison Service... The coroner has no powers to order pre-inquest disclosure. Thus, in reality, pre-inquest disclosure remains a *voluntary act*...'. (Howe, 2004, Ev. 126, emphases added)

> 'It is our experience that investigations into... prison deaths are not generally released to the family until there is a date for an inquest... Disclosure is not provided as of right, not provided early enough and is too obstructive and allows material to be kept secret... disclosure is something the family/family lawyer has to fight for... Early disclosure of custody-generated documents is vital if the family and their representatives are to have *effective and constructive participation* in the investigation'. (INQUEST, 2003b, p. 15, original emphases)

We have already addressed the related matters of statutory authority and sufficient resources that carry obvious implications for the effectiveness, or otherwise, of investigations into child deaths in penal custody. A further matter that has a direct bearing upon effectiveness, particularly in respect of family participation, is the question of openness and the disclosure of crucial information.

Thomas *et al* (2002, pp. 329-330) advise that the documents for which disclosure should be sought following a child's death in penal custody include: health care standards; the internal investigation officer's report and findings; witness statements; use of force reports (if applicable); prison adjudication and discipline documents (if applicable); suicide prevention and awareness plan documents; the child's medical records; the child's F2052SH forms and related documentation – self-harm alerts and vulnerability records – (if applicable); control and restraint manual (if applicable); wing occurrence records; any related records/reports that might be relevant (for example, pre-sentence report/s, post sentence-report, ASSET forms). Despite the reforms considered earlier, particularly with regard to the role of the Prisons and Probation Ombudsman, it remains the case that neither the child's family, nor the family's representatives (if applicable) have any automatic *statutory right* to access such documents and the extent and timing of disclosure essentially remains voluntary, conditional and subject to the vagaries of discretion.

Promptness and reasonable expedition

Investigations – unlike inquests where, as discussed later, there can be delays approaching two years – are activated immediately after a child's death in penal custody and are normally progressed without undue delay. However, this should not be taken to mean that the child's family necessarily benefits from such expeditious action. Indeed, as just noted the disclosure of investigation documents, if such disclosure is granted, is frequently delayed and in some of the more problematic cases, crucially important documents may not be made available to the child's family and their representatives (if any) until shortly before the inquest.

Transparency and integrity

'Our work establishes that at all levels state institutions are reluctant to operate mechanisms which make their regimes and practices properly accountable. Serious doubts over the effectiveness and impartiality of the investigation of cases are clear from the cases covered here. It is no reassurance to be informed that the procedures and practices of investigations are rigorous and exhaustive if their processes and reports are kept secret'. (Scraton and Chadwick, 1987b, p. 179)

'... it is the experience of many families that investigations are conducted for the convenience of the authorities and do not play any part in revealing the true circumstances'. (Liberty, 2003, p.44)

For as long as doubts and concerns in respect of the independence, effectiveness and full disclosure of investigative processes continue to prevail, the critical observations raised by Scraton and Chadwick almost twenty years ago will continue to apply. The 'guidance on disclosure', issued by the Prisons and Probation Ombudsman in March 2005 (Prisons and Probation Ombudsman for England and Wales, 2005) is, as noted, founded upon principles that are welcomed but it falls short of granting unconditional disclosure and it lacks a firm statutory footing. Ultimately, investigations following child deaths in penal custody remain, at least partially, secretive and opaque. A culture of defensiveness and mystification stubbornly confounds even the most genuine reforming effort and families, in particular, continue to be denied the right to access information and to participate fully.

Family participation

'Following a death in prison... the common experience for the bereaved is one of bemusement and bewilderment'. (Snow and McHugh, 2000, p. 144)

'The need for representation of families of those who have died in custody is not limited to appearances before inquests. Not only is there a need for such representation to be available early enough to enable adequate preparation prior to the inquest, but representation for families from the *very beginning of investigations* of deaths in custody may be an important element in enhancing the independent status of those investigations. In this respect, it is important that some mechanism is established to identify *lawyers* who are *sufficiently expert* in dealing with deaths in custody and to put families in touch with them *as soon as a death in custody occurs*. Needless to say, such representation should be made available throughout free of charge and regardless of the means of the families concerned'. (Howe, 2004, Ev. 127, emphases added)

'The relatives of the deceased are too often excluded and marginalised. To them, the investigation can often appear less a search for truth than an attempt to avoid blame, frustrate disclosure, restrict the remit of the investigation and demonise the deceased'. (INQUEST, 2003b, p.13)

By definition, investigations follow sudden and unnatural deaths for which the bereaved are singularly unprepared. At the precise point in time when an investigation commences following a child's death in penal custody, the child's family will almost certainly be experiencing a whole myriad of emotions:

profound grief; anger with state agents; confusion with unclear lines of communication and frustration with institutional insensitivity. There may also be feelings of guilt and there will almost certainly be an abiding sense of shock and disbelief. In cases when an 'investigator' – up until 2004 a representative of the very 'service' within whose 'care' the child has died – seeks the participation of the family at such an early stage of the bereavement process, it is not altogether surprising if families are unwilling, or more likely unable, to actively engage with them. The timescales are not synchronised. The public/state imperative to 'investigate' expeditiously is fundamentally at odds with the private/family need to grieve, make funeral arrangements and engage with other post-death rituals.

For the bereaved to participate in investigations to full effect, they not only need time and space, but they almost certainly require independent guidance and support from an agency such as INQUEST, together with access to expert legal advice from a specialist lawyer. Family participation at this stage of the investigation process, whether direct or indirect via a third party, can prove crucially important in shaping its terms of reference and scope. Ultimately, participation can also make the experience more bearable for the family in giving some meaning to their loss (Coles and Shaw, forthcoming, 2005). There is no *statutory duty* on the 'investigators' to advise the bereaved of the availability of such third-party expert assistance however, and despite recent progress induced by case law (see later), neither is there any *automatic right* for the family to access financial assistance in order to cover legal costs. The power relations are fundamentally distorted. The opportunities for family participation are not only impeded by the pain of bereavement therefore, they are effectively undermined by an insensitive and intrinsically unjust 'investigatory' process that is itself protected by self-interest and institutional defensiveness.

Analysing inquests

State initiative and independence

'The coronial system in the UK has many deficiencies when dealing with a death in custody [including]... the lack of independence of coroners and coronial institutions'. (Howe, 2004, Ev. 127)

'Many coroners are ill-equipped and are unaware of what is happening nationally to glean an understanding of broader policy issues surrounding deaths in custody or have not been provided with all the relevant disclosure... because they have not known what to request... This is very relevant when considering the inquest is the only public forum in which these deaths are subjected to any scrutiny and where systemic failings can be exposed... Our experience... is that lawyers representing custodial institutions... take a defensive approach to the proceedings, trying to shroud what has happened or to attack the character of the deceased rather than assisting the court in the exercise of an impartial scrutiny of the death. In addition the approach to the inquest from the authorities as a damage limitation exercise means that there has been a reluctance to learn...'. (INQUEST, 2003b, p.16)

'For many families... there is a perception that the coroner is not impartial but on the side of the authorities... In many cases this perception is reinforced throughout the inquest by the manner in which the coroner questions witnesses and allows or disallows questions from the family lawyer. The family has no right to call their own witnesses at the inquest: they can bring them to the attention of the coroner but once again the discretion rests with the coroner as to whether they should be called'. (Coles and Shaw, 2002, p.28)

'The effect of this is often to protect the interests of the powerful against the interests of the powerless'. (Ryan, 1996, p. 5)

The matter of 'state initiative' is unequivocal in respect of inquests following child deaths in prison service custody. Section 8 of the Coroners Rules imposes a statutory duty to hold an inquest before a jury. However, as noted earlier, the position regarding child deaths in Secure Training Centres is not so clear cut. Furthermore, the question of 'independence', irrespective of the site of death, is deeply problematic.

Core elements of the investigatory process that serve to undermine the very concept of independence have been considered above. Just as the 'independence' of the investigators and, more recently, the Prisons and Probation Ombudsman, can be seen to be compromised, that of the office of Coroner is – by its primary dependence on the initial investigatory process and its close working relationship with key state agencies – similarly afflicted. Equally, we have reviewed the narrow statutory confines that limit the scope of inquests, alongside the inquisitorial, as distinct from adversarial, nature of the proceedings. Inquests, therefore, fail to compensate for the intrinsic shortcomings of the initial investigations and in practice, by effectively denying independent redress, they might even serve to compound them.

It could also be argued that coroners are not appointed with sufficient powers to be truly independent to deal with controversial cases such as child deaths in penal custody and, in many cases, they also lack the necessary knowledge, skills and training. Yet, when coroners pass an opinion on the 'facts' of the case 'it carries considerable clout', they are 'the map and compass on legal direction' (Scraton, 1999, p.132). There are clear paradoxes here. At least some coroners appear to lack appropriate power, knowledge, skills, training and resources on one hand, and yet on the other they exercise significant influence. Conversely, coroners may well be all powerful with regard to the immediate inquest itself, and yet they exercise substantially less leverage over the investigatory process *per se* and they are relatively powerless, in fact, within the 'justice' system in its wider terms.

Traditionally the power of juries to frame verdicts has also been seriously circumscribed and they have been prohibited from making any independent recommendations. More recently however, two cases heard in the House of Lords, *R (Middleton) v West Somerset Coroner and R (Sacker) v West Yorkshire Coroner*, have made a significant impact regarding the role of inquest juries. The two cases were heard together over three days in February 2004. Both cases concerned adult prisoners who had hanged themselves in circumstances 'where prison officers and health care staff might have done more to prevent the death' (Cragg, 2004, p.1). On March 11 2004, the House of Lords delivered judgement in both cases and, with regard to *Middleton* in particular, a number of important statements on the law in the light of the European Convention on Human Rights and the Human Rights Act 1998 were made. This is not the place to comment on the detail of each case and such analyses are available elsewhere (see for example, Cragg, 2004; Bishop, 2004). Suffice to note that the House of Lords found that:

'An... inquest ought ordinarily to culminate in an expression, however brief, of the jury's conclusion on the disputed factual issues at the heart of the case... such as an expanded form of conclusion as to death, a narrative verdict, or by inviting answers to specific questions'. (House of Lords, cited in Bishop, 2004, p.1)

To put it another way, the Lords found that the duty to investigate extends to drawing conclusions from the investigation and inquest evidence, as to 'the accountability of the State for the death' (Cragg, 2004, p.1).

Traditionally, it might be argued that Coroners Courts and inquests have been impotent constructions: incapable of imposing independent tangible influence over the system, unable to draw and express meaningful conclusions and powerless to offer any indication of state culpability. This has led not only to the failure to learn lessons from child deaths in penal custody, but also to the failure to systematically collate, monitor and/or follow up any findings and recommendations that Coroner's might have made. The *Middleton* and *Sacker* cases represent significant developments in inquest law. They provide, at least potentially, for a greater level of independent scrutiny but, in themselves, they are unlikely to satisfy the needs of the bereaved for the truth, to unsettle the pervasive culture of individual and/or institutional impunity or to impose responsibility on the chain of command within the juvenile secure estate and the youth justice system. In this sense and irrespective of certain advances, inquests lack interventionist muscle and continue to fall short of true independence.

Effectiveness and disclosure

'There is no *mandatory* right to prior disclosure of documentation although there is a *voluntary* protocol providing for such disclosure in deaths in... prison custody. This has been a controversial issue and while there has been some reform in this area it continues to remain problematic'. (Coles and Shaw, 2002, p.27, original emphasis)

'If bereaved families feel short-changed by the... investigation, the inquest is their last resort. It inspires a belief that it is "their" inquest into the death of their loved one: "their" time, "their" right. Coroners invariably speak to the bereaved in that way, showing sympathy and concern. In their opening comments coroners also tend to emphasise that inquests set out to establish "who" died, "when", "where" and "how"... [F]amilies tend to know "who", "when" and "where". Their sole concern is "how". Yet immediately, behind the sympathetic words and sensitive acknowledgements, hangs the denial of their agenda; a spectre over the proceedings. "How" – the circumstances of death – can be pursued; it can be discussed; it should be established. But it is "how" without liability, "how" without blame. It does not take a sophisticated analysis to appreciate the contradiction'. (Scraton, 1999, p. 132)

'There are a number of respects in which an inquest may fall short... The main problem is... [that] the relevant legal provisions defining the purpose and scope of an inquest have traditionally been interpreted to mean that the inquest has a narrow fact-finding role, and does not extend to looking at the "broad circumstances" in which the death occurred'. (House of Lords House of Commons Joint Committee on Human Rights, 2004b, para. 291)

Despite various reforms, the most recent being the publication of the Prisons and Probation Ombudsman's 'guidance for disclosure' (Prisons and Probation Ombudsman for England and Wales, 2005), it continues to stand in law that the rules of procedural fairness and natural justice do not extend to an automatic *right* of disclosure for bereaved families and their legal representatives (if applicable) at inquests. Taken together with the inquisitorial imperatives that underpin inquests and their fundamentally circumscribed scope, the matters of effectiveness and disclosure raise a range of questions. Some of these questions were considered within the context of the 'Fundamental Review of Death Certification and Coroner Services' that was, as discussed earlier, established by the Home Office in July 2001. The report of the 'Fundamental Review' was published just under two years later (Home Office, 2003c) and it contained 123 recommendations

The government's response to the 'Fundamental Review' came in the form of a 'position paper' (Home Office 2004c) and was expressed 'in cautious or as yet undecided terms' indicating that 'many important decisions have yet to be taken by ministers' (Round, 2004, p. 1). Similarly, 'the timescale for implementation of [intended] reforms is unclear, as they depend in large part on the enactment of primary legislation [and]... in the past coroner reform has not been seen as a priority' (*ibid*, p.1). Despite this, the 'position paper' also signalled some support for the 'Fundamental Review' recommendations, stating that a White Paper and draft Bill on reform of the inquest system would be published in Spring 2005 (Home Office 2004c, Annex 3). Although at the time of writing, neither the White Paper nor the draft Bill have yet been published, 'reform of the coroner's system' was announced in the Queen's Speech on 17 May, 2005 (Dyer, 2005) and a Coroner Reform Bill is listed in the 2005/06 schedule of Parliamentary Business (House of Commons, 2005). However, it is still not possible to gauge either the full extent of potential reforms or their practical implications. In the meantime, the direct experiences of bereaved families continue to attest the need for more effective and wide-ranging inquests that provide them with disclosure of *all relevant* documentation well before the inquest is due; offer the prospect of truth and highlight lessons that might serve to avoid further deaths of children in penal custody:

'The death of my son has had an enormous impact on me, his brother and the rest of our family. Nothing can ever be the same again and I still feel a slow burn of anger and an overwhelming sense of injustice that will not go away. The inquest gave us some more information but did not fulfil our expectations. In many ways it led to more uncertainty and after it was over I felt as if there was no one else left to listen'.

'From the moment my son died there was a closing of ranks and a wall of silence compounded with a total lack of information... People hope for truth at the inquest, *how* the person died is already known, what they need to know is *why* and if anyone is responsible. But the present system prevents any investigation into *why*. What is needed is a legal inquiry before the inquest with a wider parameter and the opportunity for all concerned to ask and be asked questions concerning the death, along with full disclosure of official reports. The constraints of an inquest prevent this and leave most questions unanswered. Let the inquest decide *how*, let justice decide *why*'.

'The major problems with the inquest system lie in the restrictive scope in which it has to operate... There is a real need to explore liability and accountability, especially where government institutions are concerned, in order that preventive action can be taken to avoid similar events in future... In cases such as my son's there is a very clear need for open inquiries with wide-ranging remits...'. (Families cited in Coles and Shaw, 2002, pp. 60-61)

Promptness and reasonable expedition

'One of INQUEST's key concerns about the way in which deaths in custody are investigated is the serious delay from the death through to the investigation and subsequent inquests... The delay clearly causes all concerned great difficulty but this is particularly so for bereaved people who have described how their lives have been put on hold until they have been through the inquest process. INQUEST's research on families' experience of the inquest system has highlighted the detrimental effects that delays in finding out how a relative has died has placed on the physical and mental health of family members. [Furthermore]... as there is no public scrutiny of the death for such a long period, the opportunity for identifying what went wrong and to seek to prevent recurrences in the future, learning the lessons and preventing other deaths is seriously delayed'. (INQUEST, 2004c, p. 6)

'On average, inquest proceedings for death in custody cases start 1-1.5 years after a death in custody. This is a long period for a family that has turned to law looking for the truth'. (Liberty, 2003, p. 44)

'In order to assist the grieving families, guidelines should be developed to speed up the inquest process and full and prompt pre-inquest disclosure made mandatory. It is inconceivable that bereaved families are still subject to delays of over a year in trying to find out how a loved one has died'. (Howe, 2004, Ev. 127)

'We emphasise the need for the reviews of the coronial system... to address delays in the system'. (House of Lords House of Commons Joint Committee on Human Rights, 2004b, para. 304)

There is currently no statutory provision for timetabling inquests and/or for setting deadlines to reduce inordinate delays (nor is there any statutory provision for establishing how far in advance of inquests the – voluntary – disclosure of relevant documentation might be made available). Finding out how a child has died in penal custody is an essential part of the bereavement process and yet for many families this is profoundly hampered by bureaucratic delay (Davis, *et al*, 2002). By way of illustration, Joseph Scholes died, aged 16, in penal custody in March 2002 and yet his family had to wait until April 2004 for the inquest. Such delays not only hamper the extent to which lessons might be learnt and remedial action applied; they are also incompatible with the provisions of the European Convention on Human Rights and the Human Rights Act 1998; they obscure the search for truth and, perhaps most significantly, they are utterly inhumane as they serve to prolong and intensify the pain for families who have lost a child whilst in the 'care' of the state.

Transparency and integrity

'... it is perhaps worth recalling that the state enters an inquest with an enormous advantage anyway because all inquests begin with the assumption that it, or rather its employees, has no clear cut case to answer'. (Ryan, 1996, p. 164)

'The current inquest system has several flaws... There is... a lack of transparency – because disclosure is not provided as of right, it is not provided early enough and there are too many exceptions which allow material to be kept secret'. (Liberty, 2003, p. 1)

'The Coroner's inquest has become an arena for some of the most unsatisfactory rituals that follow a death – accusations, deceit, cover-up, legal chicanery, mystification; everything but a simple and uncontroversial procedure to establish the facts'. (Coles and Shaw, 2002, pp. 6-7)

'If he'd died while we were looking after him we'd have been asked questions – why weren't they'? (Bereaved family member, cited in Beckett, 1999, p. 276)

Inquests often serve to obfuscate the facts. The power relations intrinsic to the investigatory processes that follow a child's death in penal custody are fundamentally skewed; in favour of the key state agencies and to the disadvantage of the bereaved. Despite the reforms introduced by the Prisons and Probation Ombudsman (2005) the practice of discretionary and 'rationed' disclosure, and the limitations that this imposes in terms of transparency and system integrity, have endured. The devastating impact that such injustice has on the bereaved can hardly be over-stated and this is magnified in cases where families also detect distortion and deceit:

'Nothing will bring our son back sadly but we have a God-given right to know how he died. No stone should be left unturned'. (Bereaved family member, cited in Coles and Shaw, 2002, p.71)

'I cannot believe that such official and important people that I trusted before his death, to do their jobs properly and be honest, turn out to be liars; deceitful people; obstructive; economical with the truth; unsympathetic; unprofessional. Anything goes to save their hide. Anything goes to cover up the truth... I will never get over the death of my son. I will never get over the lies and cover up of my son's death. I will never trust prison staff [and] coroner's office staff again'. (Bereaved family member, *ibid*, p.62)

It is difficult to avoid the conclusion that investigations and inquests following child deaths in penal custody simply do not allow for a thorough, full and fearless inquiry, for discussion of the wider policy issues, and for accountability of those responsible at an individual and institutional level. Neither do they necessarily facilitate an honest and open approach that might help to ensure remedial action is taken to prevent future deaths in similar circumstances. In practice investigations and inquests sustain a culture of defensiveness and institutional protection.

Families are too often perceived by state agencies as simply seeking recrimination and/or financial compensation for the loss of their child. To conceptualise bereaved families by reference to mercenary and self-serving motives is itself a distortion. Whilst it is reasonable for the bereaved to seek truth and justice, Coles and Shaw (2002, p. 34) have also reported that: 'time and time again bereaved families tell us that what they want is for the inquest to result in changes which will ensure another family does not have to endure the same distressing experience'. The lack of transparency and the integrity-deficit that has typically characterised inquests following child deaths in penal custody therefore, not only raises questions in terms of compliance with the European Convention on Human Rights and the Human Rights Act 1998; it has also compounded the pain of the bereaved, undermined public confidence in state agencies and, ultimately, frustrated the prospects of preventing further deaths.

Family participation

'In a recent presentation to the Ministerial group on suicide we raised the importance of families having the opportunity of accessing *independent* advice and support at the earliest possible stage... to assist families in effectively participating in the investigation and inquest and to make it a more meaningful process... We are... concerned about the ongoing lack of equality of arms for families during the investigation and inquest process'. (INQUEST, 2004c, pp.13-14)

'Of all the issues which cause major distress, hardship and inhibition to families of people who die in controversial circumstances, the restriction on legal aid is undoubtedly the most serious in its immediate consequences... This issue has been compounded by the use of public funds [for state institutions]... Justice requires a system for granting legal aid which does not advantage one party over another'. (Scraton and Chadwick, 1987b, p.174)

'Lack of funding for families' legal assistance is a matter of particular concern ... given that funding for legal representation at the inquest is generally available to any state employees implicated in the death. The Luce Report [Home Office, 2003c] recommended that *funding for legal representation should be available to families in all cases where a public authority is also legally represented*. The Home Office [2004c] has *not undertaken to ensure this*... We recommend that, *in all cases of deaths in custody, funding for legal assistance should be provided to the next-of-kin*'. (House of Lords House of Commons Joint Committee on Human Rights, 2004b, para. 309, emphases added)

The concerns already raised with regard to the limited 'independence' and 'effectiveness' of inquest processes, their circumscribed scope, ongoing limitations with regard to disclosure and transparency, the protracted bureaucratic proceedings and long delays all combine to seriously impede family participation. Such phenomena symbolise an outmoded administrative mindset that serves to marginalise bereaved families from the very investigatory processes within which they should be treated as central 'players'. Whilst it is important to recognise that recent reforms have sought to soften some of the hardest edges in the legal process following child deaths in penal custody, and some individual Coroners try to be sensitive to families' feelings and concerns (Davis *et al*, 2002), ultimately the legal-administrative apparatus fails to facilitate family participation (Coles and Shaw, 2002). This is evident across the whole range of overlapping and intersecting investigatory and inquest processes as we have discussed, but two manifestations are particularly noteworthy.

First, further to notifying a family of a child's death in penal custody there is no statutory *duty* requiring any state agency (including the Prison Service, the Prisons and Probation Ombudsman or the Youth Justice Board) to direct the family towards *independent* support, advice and representation. This is problematic and difficult to understand. It could also be easily remedied if the key state agencies routinely referred families to the expert casework, advice and support services that INQUEST can provide, for example. The case for making such referrals is unequivocal, not least because most families have no developed knowledge of investigatory and inquest processes (Davis *et al*, 2002). By way of illustration, INQUEST surveyed 130 families that had used its services between 1997 and 2000. Of the families surveyed 75 per cent had no knowledge at all with regard to the inquest system and, although there was some variation within the remaining 25 per cent, most had 'very little' knowledge (Coles and Shaw, 2002. See also Coles and Shaw, forthcoming, 2005). Such families, at a time of profound shock and grief, are effectively denied support and the consequences can be very serious. They are invariably completely unaware of their legal rights and understandably mystified by the formal investigatory processes. In such circumstances the notion of 'family participation' is extremely remote.

Second, further institutionalised obstacles to participation are encountered by families who seek financial support to commission legal representation. Indeed, there are no statutory provisions that allow a *guaranteed* right to *non-means tested* public funding (legal aid) in respect of representation in coroners courts. The absence of *automatic* public funding in such circumstances (criticised as far back as 1971 – see Home Office, 1971), together with families' consequent difficulties in securing expert and specialist legal representation, serves to 'fuel bereaved families' suspicions of cover-up and generally to increase their feelings of frustration and helplessness' (Snow and McHugh, 2000, p. 146). There is an established and contested history to this.

The Legal Aid and Advice Act 1949 and its successor Act, the Legal Aid Act 1974, made provision for regulations to be laid before parliament by the Lord Chancellor, allowing legal aid for inquests, but no such provisions were ever put in place. Moreover, as Thomas *et al* (2002, p. 120) have noted: 'the third Act of Parliament dealing with legal aid, the Legal Aid Act 1988, was silent on the issue'. The Access to Justice Act 1999 (implemented in April 2000) maintained the *general exclusion* of inquests from legal aid. The same Act however, also opened the door to legal aid under its '*exceptional funding*' provisions. Applications for funding made under such provisions are referred by the Legal Services Commission (LSC) to the Lord Chancellor for approval or otherwise. Funding might be granted if one of two 'exceptional circumstances' tests are met: either, that the case involves a 'significant wider public interest' or, that the case provides an 'overwhelming importance to the client'. Such provisions have given rise to a 'legal aid maze' (Bawdon, 2003, p.7), not least because the Lord Chancellor made it clear (in revised guidance issued in November 2001) that the 'exceptional circumstances' tests are intended to be set at a high level.

In February 2004, the Lord Chancellor issued further 'draft guidance on when it may be appropriate for public funding to be provided for legal representation at inquests' (Department of Constitutional Affairs, 2004, p.2). The revised guidance was precipitated by two appeal court rulings in October 2003 in the cases of *R (Amin) v Secretary of State for the Home Department and R (Khan) v Secretary of State for Health*. In the case of *Amin* the Lords of Appeal ruled that the State's duty to investigate the death of a prisoner in its custody was not discharged unless there was an *appropriate* level of participation by the next of kin. In the case of *Khan* the Court of Appeal (Civil Division) further established that public funding for an inquest was to be available to the bereaved relatives where the death was caused by an agent of the State. In both cases the Courts considered Article 2 of the European Convention on Human Rights to be engaged.

Again, taking account of *Amin* and *Khan* and in accordance with the Community Legal Service (Financial) (Amendment No. 2) Regulations, the Lord Chancellor, from December 2003, has had the power to waive the upper eligibility limit for public funding in deaths in custody cases. This power applies where it is 'unreasonable to expect [the] wider family to bear the full cost of the hearing' but it does no preclude 'requests for a contribution from the... wider family' (Department of Constitutional Affairs, 2004, p.1). Furthermore, the amendments initially contained within the 2004 draft guidance, extend the 'exceptional funding' provisions of the Access to Justice Act 1999. Whilst all of this is welcome however, families access to public funding ultimately remains contingent and conditional, subject to 'tests' and always requiring justification.

In the final analysis, the ability of families to participate in investigations and inquests following deaths of children in penal custody continues to be undermined by way of deliberate institutional obstacles. Advances have certainly been made, due primarily to the struggles of families themselves alongside non-governmental organisations and human rights advocates. Despite progress however, investigations and inquests do not comprise 'level playing fields' and the seemingly unlimited public resources available to state agencies in protecting their interests, outweigh substantially the constrained funds available to families in their search for truth and justice.

Chapter 5
Key Conclusions and Recommendations

'... [M]ore generally, the Committee is deeply concerned at the high increasing numbers of children in custody... The Committee is also extremely concerned at the conditions that children experience in detention... and that children do not receive adequate protection or help... noting the very poor staff-child ratio, high levels of violence, bullying, self harm and suicide'. (United Nations Committee on the Rights of the Child, 2002, para. 57)

'...[G]reater use of custody for juveniles is made in England and Wales than in most other industrialised, democratic countries'. (Youth Justice Board for England and Wales, 2004, para. 9)

'Given this shift towards greater use of imprisonment, it seems highly unlikely that the incidence of custodial deaths... will be significantly reduced'. (Howe, 2004, Ev. 126)

Introduction

This book is rooted in critical analysis. Chapter 1 described the background, the principal objectives and the primary research methods upon which the book is based. Chapter 2 traced the key shifts in contemporary youth justice law and policy that have underpinned penal expansion and, accordingly, have produced a substantial increase in the number of child prisoners in England and Wales. Such developments are located within a highly politicised context in which punitive imperatives and 'toughness' priorities pay scant regard to research evidence, practical experience or criminological rationality. The practices of child incarceration continue to expose damaged children to damaging environments, at great public expense and massive human cost, with virtually no positive return when measured in terms of crime prevention and community safety. Chapter 3 situated the analysis of child deaths alongside a detailed review of policy and practice responses. We have argued that in detaining increasing numbers of children, at younger ages and for longer terms, in manifestly unsafe penal environments, the state fails in its duty of care. Between July 1990 and January 2005, such failure produced fatal outcomes for 28 children. Each of the key state agencies express commitment to avoid further child deaths in penal custody, but the evidence continues to imply, despite the various reforms reviewed here, that such an objective is unlikely to be realised in present circumstances. Chapter 4 examined the investigatory processes and inquests that are implemented when children die as a result of the above failures. Paradoxically, as we have seen, such processes have also failed: they are deeply problematic and inadequate.

Numerous conclusions and recommendations are contained within the body of the book, some implicit within the overall analysis and others are more explicitly stated. It is not our intention to systematically reiterate these here. Indeed, it is not our objective to produce an extended list of 'micro' recommendations, not least because such lists have been expertly presented elsewhere (see for example, Coles and Shaw, 2002; Thomas et al, 2002; Home Office 2003c; Liberty 2003; House of Lords House of Commons Joint Committee on Human Rights, 2004b; Scraton and Moore, 2004). Given that this book comprises the first detailed analysis of child deaths in penal custody in England and Wales, however, it is important to conclude by drawing out the key lessons and 'macro' recommendations. We therefore focus upon a sequence of four sets of related and overlapping conclusions and recommendations that, taken together distil the underpinning messages of the book.

Children, damage and penal regimes: a case for abolition

Conclusions

> 'There is no doubt that some of the most vulnerable people in the country are to be found in our prisons... There is no doubt also, that distress caused by detention adds to these vulnerabilities'. (House of Lords House of Commons Joint Committee on Human Rights, 2004b, para. 368)

> 'It is difficult to convey to a public, largely ignorant of the true nature of the modern prison and sometimes coached by the media to regard it as a soft and benevolent setting, that prison is still a place where people suffer extremes of desperation and despair'. (Medlicott, 2001, p. 9)

'Horrible, it's just horrible. That's all I can say. That's the only way I can explain it'. (Child prisoner, aged 16 years, cited in Goldson, 2002b, p.132)

'The pains of imprisonment are many and varied. They are also, often, hidden. It is not to the visible eye or the measuring instrument that they are perceptible, but to the "informed heart"... The evidence suggests that the pains of imprisonment are tragically underestimated... some prisons may contain "invitations to suicide"'. (Liebling, 1998, p. 66 and p. 73)

Explaining why some child prisoners end their lives in penal custody, others 'survive' despite being emotionally, psychologically and/or physically damaged to varying degrees, and a further group, almost certainly a minority, appear to 'do their time' comparatively unscathed, is extraordinarily complex, if at all possible. Although it seems likely that there is some relation between what Liebling (2004) terms 'imported vulnerability' on the one hand, and institutionally-imposed vulnerability on the other or, to put it another way, an association between 'innate' and 'structural'/'contextual' vulnerability (Goldson, 2002b), the precise nature of such intersections are far from clear (Medlicott, 2001).

What is clear, however, is that official discourse tends to privilege constructions of individual pathology ('imported' or 'innate' vulnerability), whilst negating the significance of damaging penal regimes (institutionally-, structurally- or contextually-imposed vulnerabilities). Within such discourses, therefore, 'failure to cope' is primarily interpreted by reference to the individual 'weakness' and 'inadequacy' of child prisoners, rather than being seen as a consequence of inappropriate treatment and conditions within penal custody. Ultimately, this is a distorted rationale that allows the state and its agencies to minimise – if not deny – responsibility and accountability, whilst effectively 'blaming' child prisoners for their own death and/or damage. It is dishonest and ethically reprehensible.

Despite, the various policy and procedural reforms that have been, and continue to be, implemented and the determined practical efforts of some operational staff to take account of the specific needs of child prisoners, penal custody remains an unsuitable environment for children. The ever-increasing application of 'assessment tools' perpetuates the conceptual emphasis on the 'vulnerabilities' specific to individual children, as distinct from the intrinsic problems of penal regimes. Furthermore, in practice such 'assessments' often comprise little more than technical procedural processing (Goldson, 2002b). Irrespective of reform efforts therefore, and no matter how the practices of institutional detention are 'dressed up', to punish a child by way of incarceration is to impose 'organised hurt' (Hentig, 1937) and in current conditions this is often tantamount to institutionalised abuse.

Notwithstanding the best efforts of those staff who are motivated to do so, 'caring' for children in penal custody, especially Young Offender Institutions, is an almost impossible task. Three factors are particularly significant. First, there is the question of values, roles and responsibilities and the tensions and contradictions therein. In the final analysis, the priority role of staff is to maintain discipline, order and institutional security. Set against this is the duty of care. This incongruous duality of controlling and caring functions is the source of conceptual ambiguity and operational difficulty and the care principle is always relegated to a secondary status. Second, there is the question of limited resources and relatively low staffing levels, that tend to prohibit any meaningful engagement between staff and child prisoners beyond the basic routines of day-to-day operations. Third, there is the question of staff training. It goes almost without saying that expertly developed and refined knowledge and skills, together with ongoing professional training, is required to meet the complex needs of child prisoners. However, this is not available for staff working with children in any form of penal custody, particularly prison custody. Although 'training' consistently features prominently within official discourse, policy statements and institutional 'mission statements', in reality its delivery is patchy, inconsistent and superficial. Ten years ago Goldson (1995) identified serious training deficits amongst staff working in local authority secure units (now termed secure children's homes). More recently, Her Majesty's Inspector of Prisons (2005, p.59) has referred to 'concerns' with regard to 'the absence of sufficient training for staff' working with child prisoners and has observed that, although 'the Prison Service has now developed a training package... it lasts for only seven days and, even then, establishments are expressing concern about how they will facilitate this'. Furthermore, 'training in suicide and self-harm is no longer mandatory [and while] some prisons keep up to date with training... others had done none in the previous year or failed to meet targets' (*ibid*, p.18). In essence, staff are required to fulfil a function for which they are neither professionally trained nor adequately equipped.

The difficulties presented by the above are additionally compounded by a problematic cocktail of overcrowding (a direct consequence of punitive policy and penal expansion) and staff shortages (arguably accentuated by absences due to stress and work-related ill-health. See Prison Reform Trust, 2004b). When penal custody is pressured in this way 'services which have been put in place to support vulnerable [children] become overwhelmed with the result that some [children] cannot access support when they need it. Staff who are overstretched can fail to notice when [a child] is experiencing distress' (Mind, 2004, Ev. 108). Bullying is a primary source of such 'distress' for children in penal custody. Moreover, bullying in all of its forms, physical assault, sexual assault, verbal abuse, intimidation, extortion, and theft, is endemic, particularly in Young Offender Institutions (Goldson, 2002b). It is no surprise, therefore, that many child prisoners live with the constant spectre of fear and an enduring feeling of being 'unsafe' (Challen and Walton, 2004; Her Majesty's Chief Inspector of Prisons, 2005). This, in turn, is thought to heighten the risk of damage and/or death:

> 'Feeling unsafe or fearful may also contribute to suicide... particularly if prisoners do not see any other way out of a situation where they are being bullied, threatened etc'. (Mills, 2004, Ev. 130)

Indeed, the absence of 'any other way out' is a crucial factor here because, in practice, there is nowhere for a child prisoner to go. Children who report bullying, or who express distress, 'invite' scorn from other child prisoners *and* from staff. On the one hand, the compelling 'anti-grassing' ethic, coupled with the self-defeating consequences of being labelled a 'grass', effectively silences the bullied child prisoner. On the other hand, communicating serious distress, self-harming or even attempting self-inflicted death, can be cynically interpreted by staff as manipulative, rather than as desperate:

> '... self-harm or suicide attempts are sometimes seen by staff... as manipulative, attention-seeking, "gestures" which are deliberately carried out by prisoners for their own gain such as to obtain transfer to a better setting, escape problems with others or be given a phone call to loved ones. Such attitudes may lead staff to dismiss the severity of the prisoner's distress and they may be treated with contempt and disapproval rather than support and help'. (Mills, 2004, Ev. 130).

The prospect of being met with 'contempt and disapproval' effectively serves to gag child prisoners, thus leaving them alone with their pain.

Liebling (2004) has recently reported that the most significant indicators of the 'moral performance' of penal institutions include: 'respect, humanity, relationships, trust, fairness, order, safety and well-being'. The same 'dimensions' are also thought to provide the safest penal environments. The experiences of children in penal custody are often characterised by fundamentally different 'dimensions', however. Lack of 'care'; under-qualified and over-stretched staff; cultures of violence, intimidation and bullying; prevalent racism, sexism and homophobia; omnipresent fear and anxiety; penal regimes that provide only minimal and wholly inadequate 'safeguards' – these are the realities of life inside for many children in penal custody. The degradation, the claustrophobia, the denial of 'childhood', the emptiness of time and the fear of place corrodes and crushes the child's sense of self. This eclipses reform and all of its rhetorical 'safer custody' claims. Ultimately, this is the 'invitation to suicide'.

Recommendations

'The imprisonment of such vulnerable people is at the root of the problem itself. It is not only that this incarceration is senseless, but that it is in fact the first step on a path that can lead to self-inflicted death...'. (House of Lords House of Commons Joint Committee on Human Rights, 2004b, para. 372)

'A reduction in the numbers being held in prisons [and other forms of penal custody] in England and Wales is imperative in order to prevent a further rise in self-inflicted deaths'. (Prison Reform Trust, 2004b, Ev. 116)

'Deaths in custody are best avoided by our taking an abolitionist stance... All deaths in custody will best be avoided by our employing *the minimum use of custody*...'. (Morgan, 1996, p. 22, original emphasis)

We fully endorse these statements. It is a measure of the depth of the 'new punitiveness' (Goldson, 2002a) evident throughout contemporary youth justice law and policy in England and Wales, however, that penal reduction and/or abolition is not on the political agenda. This is despite the deaths of 28 children in penal custody and the damage imposed upon literally thousands more. Instead, each of the major political parties continue to commit themselves to ever 'tougher' policies (Liberal Democratic Party, 2004; Conservative Party, 2005; Labour Party, 2005), whilst the Youth Justice Board for England and Wales (2004a, paras. 10-11) rather lamely refers to an 'aspirational' strategy whereby 'all institutions within the secure estate for juveniles should have a child-centred culture'. The glaring contradiction illuminated by a continued political commitment to punitive 'toughness' and a naive 'aspiration' towards 'caring custody', is self-evident. A fundamental change of direction is required.

Policy-makers within core state agencies are not obliged to keep record numbers of children in penal custody, exposing them to the dangerous regimes discussed throughout this book. They choose to do so. Moreover, they make this choice in the knowledge that it is irrational when measured in terms of crime prevention and community safety. Pretending that penal custody might one day be 'child-centred', is no substitute for engaging with a determined and strategically applied policy of penal reduction. We concur with Rod Morgan, ironically now the Chairperson of the Youth Justice Board for England and Wales, that an 'abolitionist stance' necessitating the minimum use of custody, provides the most effective means of safeguarding child 'offenders'. We further contend, on the basis of the evidence presented here and elsewhere (Goldson, 2001b; Nacro, 2005), that the same approach will also deliver the most effective results in terms of youth crime prevention and community safety.

We recommend therefore, the abolition of the use of *all* Prison Service and Private Sector custody for child 'offenders', and only the minimum use of Local Authority Secure Children's Home provision for children whose behaviour places themselves and/or others at *demonstrable serious risk*. In cases where children are deprived of their liberty 'as a measure of last resort and for the shortest appropriate period of time' (United Nations General Assembly, 1989, Article 37b), the full weight of all relevant international human/children's rights standards, treaties, rules and conventions should, of necessity, apply as minimum and non-negotiable safeguards.

We realise that the abolition of the use of penal custody for children is unlikely to be implemented with immediate effect. Thus we offer two supplementary recommendations. First, as the initial stage of a wider abolitionist programme, that a determined and ambitious strategy of penal reduction be introduced without delay. Second, pending complete abolition, that the subsequent recommendations in this concluding chapter be implemented forthwith.

From fragmentation to coherence: a case for a comprehensive review

Conclusions

> 'The fact that every death in custody brings into question the legitimacy/illegitimacy and efficiency/inefficiencies of the particular custodial system is something which modern judicial authorities have refused to accept as an unassailable starting point'. (Thomas et al, 2002, p.26)

> 'It is difficult to convey, without multiplying case histories *ad nauseam*, the exasperation we feel as inquest after inquest, year after year, reveals

the same administrative and medical blunders, the same failures of communication, the same almost wilful blindness to prisoners' distress... it is true in too many cases, and the lessons of these cases do not seem to be learned'. (Coles and Ward, 1994, p. 142)

'There is a failure to learn lessons from deaths because the findings and recommendations of coroners are not published, and these recommendations are not monitored or followed up in any systematic way'. (Liberty, 2003, p.2)

The emphasis on individualised constructions of pathology ('imported' or 'innate' vulnerability), 'failure to cope', 'weakness' and 'inadequacy', serves not only to divert attention from inappropriate penal regimes, state responsibility and accountability, but it also fragments understanding of the commonalities of circumstance that characterise child deaths in penal custody. As explained in Chapter 4, the question of 'how' an individual child came by their death in penal custody, the primary preoccupation of investigations and inquests, is by definition circumscribed. It is essentially confined to an individual child in a given penal institution at a specific moment in time. It is necessarily abstracted from analysis of youth justice policy and/or any consideration of the wider social, structural, material and institutional arrangements that defined the child's circumstances prior to death. If such deliberate and institutionalised circumscription obscures understanding of individual child deaths in penal custody, it also completely negates the combined and/or collective lessons that might otherwise be drawn from an aggregated understanding of multiple cases.

That the Coroner's Court is a court of limited record, as distinct from a court of full and frank inquiry, is itself problematic. With regard to moving beyond the obfuscation of truth and the fragmentation of learning, towards a more comprehensive and coherent understanding, two further obstacles exist. First, the findings and recommendations of coroners and juries following inquests into child deaths in penal custody are not published. Second, given the non-publication of findings and recommendations, they cannot be systematically analysed, monitored or followed-up. The primary consequence, is that it is not possible to undertake a detailed and aggregated analysis of the 28 child deaths in penal custody. It follows, therefore, that the lessons that might be learned from such an analysis, together with the benefit that could ensue from their application, continue to elude.

Despite this, it is not impossible to define a range of features that consistently emerge with regard to child deaths in penal custody:

- Multiple and inter-locking modes of disadvantage that beset child prisoners.
- A relational 'pathway' between public care and penal custody for significant numbers of child prisoners.
- System strain as a result of hardening policy responses to child offenders and penal expansion, including: overcrowding, hastily implemented and thus incomplete 'assessments' and competing operational pressures that fundamentally compromise the 'duty of care'.
- 'Placements' in penal custody that are not only unsuitable in nature but are also inappropriate by location. In other words, manifestly 'vulnerable' children detained in Prison Service institutions and children 'placed' at great distance from their home area thus rendering regular family visits near impossible.
- Inadequate intra-agency and inter-agency communication and information exchange.
- Hostile institutional cultures predicated upon bullying and intimidation.
- The institutional (mis)conceptualisation of 'need' as 'manipulation'.
- The corrosive impact of penal custody on child prisoners.
- Persistent problems associated with the physical infrastructure of penal custody, particularly Prison Service custody, including cell design and access to ligature points.
- Poor medical care and limited access to specialist 'therapeutic' services.
- A failure to implement suicide prevention guidelines.
- The intrinsic degradation imposed by institutional responses to 'vulnerable' child prisoners, including the use of 'strip' conditions, isolation and surveillance (as distinct from watchful care).
- Continuing deficits in terms of openness, transparency, rigour and independence with regard to investigative processes following child deaths in penal custody.
- The institutionalised marginalistion of the bereaved and the inequality of arms between state agencies and families.

In combination, such features can be lethal, and their recurrent nature gives rise to the 'exasperation' to which Coles and Ward (1994, p.142) have referred. The need to learn from this is compelling.

Recommendations

'The problem of deaths in custody has not been neglected by government or public bodies. Evidence to this inquiry has detailed a wealth of initiatives which have sought to research and address aspects of the problem... However, these disparate initiatives have not been effective in tackling the scale of the problem... Greater urgency in eliminating bad practice and spreading good practice throughout these institutions is badly needed. In numerous cases the issues surrounding deaths in custody are similar'. (House of Lords House of Commons Joint Committee on Human Rights, 2004b, para. 374)

'Recommendations must be a regular component of the inquest verdict. These must be published, their implementation must be monitored, and a publicly accessible data base must be created'. (Liberty, 2003, p.4)

At the level of each individual case, the circumstances leading to a child's death in penal custody might appear to comprise a sequence of exceptional 'mistakes' and abnormal 'misunderstandings'. By definition, the atypical nature of child death implies that, however unfortunate and regrettable, little more could have been done. The claimed legitimacy, efficiency and integrity of penal custody remains undisturbed. Wider questions of policy are not raised. At the level of aggregated cases, however, when account is taken of the commonalities of circumstance that characterise the 28 child deaths, it is no longer possible to conceive such deaths as isolated and unconnected aberrations. Indeed, the consistent features and intersecting similarities of such cases illustrate the systemic failings that continue to be produced and reproduced through the practices and processes of child incarceration. It is here that questions of legitimacy, efficiency and integrity with regard to penal custody and youth justice policy become more contested.

The fact that despite certain advances in investigation and inquest procedures, the findings and (in some cases) recommendations that emerge from individual cases are neither published nor monitored remains problematic. Similarly, the failure of state agencies to collate a systematic and aggregated analysis of the broad circumstances that give rise to child deaths in penal custody is questionable. This might well insulate the practice of placing children in penal custody from searching questions and, in so doing, preserve the appearance of 'legitimacy' and 'efficiency'. However, it also serves to fragment knowledge, to dissipate lessons and to undermine a coherent understanding of child deaths. Ultimately, it dilutes the penal system's capacity to safeguard children.

We recommend that measures should be implemented to: investigate the policy contexts and commonalities of circumstance that characterise child deaths in penal custody by means of a comprehensive and thorough review; learn and apply the lessons gleaned from such a review; routinely publish findings and recommendations from individual inquests and systematically monitor the implementation of the same. The formation of a robust *independent* body will be necessary in order to facilitate the implementation of such measures.

Towards independent comprehensive analysis and intervention: a case for a 'Standing Commission on Custodial Deaths'

Conclusions

> 'In concluding we want to reiterate our view that a Standing Commission on Custodial Deaths be set up which would bring together the evidence collected from the separate bodies in place to investigate deaths in custodial settings. Our monitoring of deaths in custody this year further illustrates... the failure of the State to learn the lessons arising from the cases and the lack of joined-up thinking between government agencies. Such a Commission could play a key role in the promotion of a culture of human rights and promote measures to prevent or minimise the risk of future violations of Article 2 of the Human Rights Act'. (INQUEST, 2004c, p.19)

> 'Our principal conclusion is therefore that there is a need for a central forum to address the significant national problem of deaths in custody... a permanent body, with a remit to address all aspects of deaths in custody, is required'. (House of Lords House of Commons Joint Committee on Human Rights, 2004b, para. 375)

The need for the establishment of an independent body, possibly a 'Standing Commission', in order to systematically address the question of deaths in custody in general, and child deaths in particular, is self-evident to many. For our purposes here, we are primarily concerned with the latter and, as such, we tailor our conclusions and recommendations accordingly.

As explained above, there are many common concerns that link together individual child deaths, just as there are issues that transcend the narrowly focused remits of specific government departments and state agencies. A 'Standing Commission on Custodial Deaths' would serve to look beyond individual cases and/or particular state agencies, therefore, and engage with child deaths in penal custody on a more holistic or collective basis. The 'Commission' might collect, collate, analyse and publish findings in respect of child deaths, identify common issues, develop programmes of research and – pending the abolition of the use of Prison Service and Private Sector custody for children – assist in the development and delivery of 'best practice' in safeguarding children and promoting the 'duty of care'. We do not anticipate the 'Commission' reproducing the work of other investigatory bodies, although we would expect it to be empowered statutorily to intervene in individual inquests where appropriate as an 'interested party'. We envisage an active interventionist role for the 'Commission', therefore, underpinned by the power to hold a wider inquiry and to summon witnesses in circumstances where there might be a consistent pattern of deaths, as in the case of child deaths in penal custody.

Recommendations

'[W]e recommend the setting up of a Standing Commission on Custodial Deaths... Such an over-arching body could identify key issues and problems arising out of the investigation and inquest process following deaths and it would monitor the outcomes and progress of any recommendations. It could also look at serious incidents of self-harm or near deaths in custody where there is a need to review and identify any lessons. Arising from this it would develop policy and research, disseminate findings where appropriate and encourage collaborative working... It would play a key role in the promotion of a culture of human rights in regard to the protection of people in custody'. (INQUEST, 2003a, p.4)

'Such a body would need to include representation of community and other interested groups and it should certainly not seek to displace them'. (Howe, 2004, Ev. 128)

We endorse each of these recommendations and urge that they should be applied to child deaths in penal custody as a matter of urgency. The principal advantage of such a 'Commission' over existing remedies, is that its power and scope would not necessarily be limited to individual child deaths in penal custody. Whilst not neglecting the significance and specificities of such cases, the 'Commission' would also aim to identify the commonalities within, across and between cases. Its focus would also, of necessity, be fixed on child welfare and youth justice policy in its broadest applications and, more particularly the law and policies that govern the question of child imprisonment. In this sense, we might anticipate that the 'Commission' would lend its authority – grounded in comprehensive, careful and considered analysis – to the case for the abolition of the use of *all* Prison Service and Private Sector custody for child 'offenders', and only the minimum use of Local Authority Secure Children's Home provision for children whose behaviour places themselves and/or others at *proven serious risk*.

The death of Joseph Scholes: a case for a public inquiry

Conclusions

'Our verdict is accidental death, in part contributed because the risk was not properly recognised or appropriate precautions were not taken to prevent it... Do we consider that there has been a failure in the system?... Yes, we do'. (The Foreman of the Jury recounting the verdict at the conclusion of the inquest into the death of Joseph Scholes, Shrewsbury Coroner's Court, April 30, 2004)

'Joseph's death raises a number of wider questions about the treatment and care of children in the criminal justice system and the accountability of those agencies responsible, in particular the Youth Justice Board, the Prison Service and Social Services Departments. It asks questions of society and how it should respond when children show clear signs of being disturbed and in need of professional intervention. It raises questions about how agencies and individuals could have intervened in Joseph's case and how we can ensure that we have better systems and better practice in the future... A public inquiry into a case like Joseph's would be able to examine the fundamental flaws in our system for dealing with children who break the law'. (INQUEST, 2003b, p.7)

'... it concerns us as a society, for if Joe's death does anything, it throws an unwelcome spotlight on our appetite for punishment, for seeing it inflicted, for tolerating its severity, on our apparent ease of consigning those like Joe to the far reaches of our consciousness, where they are neither seen nor heard... Some might complain that this is too bleak a view, but were it otherwise, Joseph Scholes would not have died, alone and frightened, hanging from the bars of a cell window'. (Bennett, 2004, p. 1)

We have discussed the circumstances that led to the death of Joseph Scholes, aged 16 years, in some detail in Chapter 3. Joseph hanged himself from the bars of his cell in Stoke Heath Young Offenders Institution on March 24, 2002. He had only been at Stoke Heath for nine days during which time he had experienced treatment described at the inquest as 'dehumanising'.

In November 2003 Joseph's mother, Yvonne Scholes, together with INQUEST and Nacro (a national 'crime reduction agency') launched a call in the House of Commons for a public inquiry into his death. The call was almost immediately supported by over 100 MPs and Peers, many other individuals in public life and a wide range of penal reform, child welfare and human rights organisations and agencies (INQUEST and Nacro, 2004).

The inquest into Joseph's death was held in April 2004 and it extended over two weeks. The inquest was characterised by best practice within the imposed limitations and confines examined in chapter 4. It benefited from the thorough preparation and expertly executed representation provided by the legal team acting for Yvonne Scholes, together with an extremely conscientious coroner and an attentive inquest jury that offered a detailed narrative verdict. The inquest concluded with the Coroner taking exceptional action in writing to the Home Secretary and recommending a full public inquiry.

Two months later, in June 2004, Chris Ruane MP tabled an Early Day Motion in Parliament:

> '... [T]his House... notes despite being recognised by all concerned as a deeply disturbed child he was allocated to Prison Service accommodation without the standards of care needed for such a vulnerable child... and therefore calls upon the Government to set up a comprehensive public inquiry to deal with the many issues concerning Joseph's death so that lessons can be learnt about the treatment of children in the criminal justice system'. (Cited in INQUEST, 2004c, pp. 2-3)

Also in June 2004, Lord Navnit Dholakia, supported by Baroness Stern and Baroness Howe, raised the matter in the House of Lords and the Right Reverend Tim Stevens did likewise at the Church of England's General Synod. In the period between November 2003 and June 2004, therefore, substantial support for a public inquiry into the death of Joseph Scholes was expressed within both Houses of Parliament, the General Synod of the Church of England, the Coroner's Court and from a wide range of leading child welfare and penal reform agencies, prominent individuals in public life and national experts in youth justice.

The government's initial response to such an authoritative call was disappointing. In fact for many months the government made no response at all, either to the initiative taken by Yvonne Scholes, INQUEST and Nacro in November 2003, or to the Coroner's recommendation of April 2004. In June 2004, however, after support for a public inquiry had further been expressed in both Houses of Parliament and the General Synod of the Church of England, Baroness Scotland, Minister of State at the Home Office, eventually confirmed that:

> 'The coroner has written to my right honourable friend the Home Secretary, commenting on a number of issues arising from the inquest.

We are considering his comments and will reply in due course. We will make known our response by means of a Ministerial Statement'. (Cited in INQUEST, 2004c, p. 3)

After this statement the government remained silent until Yvonne Scholes' legal representatives indicated that she would take legal action. On September 16, 2004, therefore, the final day prior to the Parliamentary recess, INQUEST, Joseph's family and their legal representatives were informed, by a member of the press, that a negative decision regarding the call for a public inquiry had been announced in Parliament. The delay in reaching this decision, together with the means by which it was communicated, can only be described as contemptuous.

The 'story' did not end in September 2004, however. In December 2004, the House of Lords House of Commons Joint Committee on Human Rights (2004b) noted the substantial support for the call for a public inquiry and, moreover, it added its own support:

> 'This is a call that we support. There has never been a public inquiry into the death of a child in custody. We recommend that the Home Secretary orders a public inquiry into the death of Joseph Scholes in order that lessons can be fully learnt from the circumstances that led up to his tragic death'. (*ibid*, para. 75)

Despite all of this, in March 2005 the Government (House of Lords House of Commons Joint Committee on Human Rights, 2005, p.7) again stated its opposition to a public inquiry, arguing that it 'was unlikely to bring to light any additional factors not already uncovered in the earlier investigations'.

The inadequacy of the Government's response was noted by Baroness Stern in June 2005:

> 'It is a matter of great regret to me, and no doubt to other noble Lords, that the recommendation of the committee [Joint Committee of Human Rights] that a public inquiry should be held into Joseph's death, was not accepted by the Government, especially since three more children, aged respectively 14, 15 and 16, have died in our custody—that is, the custody of our state—since Joseph died.' (Hansard, Column 1038, June 9 2005)

Most significant of all, on 13 June 2005 Yvonne Scholes was granted permission to judicially review the Government's refusal to allow a public inquiry into his death. The Judge, in recognising the public importance of the case, granted expedition and the judicial review will be heard later in 2005.

Recommendations

'... I have powers under the Coroner's Rules to make recommendations and I am going to exercise that power in this case and I publicly announce now that I will be writing to the Home Secretary and I shall be writing in these terms. Not only should you know that I am writing to him, you should know the substance of what I am writing to him and I am bringing to his attention the circumstances and issues arising out of the death of the late Joseph Scholes... I shall be informing him that many issues were raised and investigated: whilst sentencing policy was outside the scope of the inquest, the two year detention and training order that Joseph received was part of the chain of events culminating in his death... Without going behind the sentence Joseph received at this inquest, it seems to me essential that there is an urgent and comprehensive review... It seemed that there was an element of chance in the allocation process in that on one particular day a place might be available for a vulnerable child and he (typically a 15 or 16 year old boy) may receive a place [in a Local Authority Secure Children's Home as distinct from Prison Service custody], but on the next day a similar child with the same needs would not... It seemed clear to me that the allocation of vulnerable young children... should be determined on a needs basis and not on a resources basis... In all the circumstances, and so that the review can include sentencing policy, which is an essential ingredient but outside the scope of this Inquest, I consider that the review should take the form of a Public Inquiry when all interested persons can make their view known. It should also include consideration of the safe cell clothing which Joseph wore for the first four days, day and night, with no underwear, and which was stated to be for his self-protection... but was also described... as dehumanising'. (The Coroner's concluding remarks at the inquest into the death of Joseph Scholes, Shrewsbury Coroner's Court, April 30, 2004)

We reiterate the call for a full public inquiry into the circumstances that led to the death of Joseph Scholes. The Government's decision to consistently resist allowing such an inquiry runs counter to the spirit of democratic accountability, transparency and the pressing need to learn from the 'failure in the system' that cost a 16-year-old child his life. Accordingly, we recommend as a matter of urgency, that the Government should re-consider its decision and implement a comprehensive public inquiry.

For reasons that have been examined in some detail throughout this book, the current inquest system, together with associated investigatory processes, are incapable of dealing with the systemic issues highlighted in the case of Joseph Scholes. In fact it is a system that fails. It fails the legacy of the children whose lives have been lost in penal custody. It fails the families of these children. It fails the wider public interest in denying opportunities to ensure that lessons are learnt and future fatalities might be avoided. Given the range of state agencies involved in Joseph's 'care'; the breadth, depth and complexity of the issues involved; the narrow and necessarily prohibitive confines of the coronial system; the State's obligations as provided by the European Convention on Human Rights and the Human Rights Act and the State's fundamental 'duty of care', only a public inquiry will suffice.

End Note

In some important ways our conclusions and recommendations reiterate those reached by a range of authoritative bodies. They are also clearly linked. The implementation of such recommendations requires substantial reform and resolute determination from those with power and responsibility. A full public inquiry into the circumstances leading to the death of Joseph Scholes might be an effective starting point of a process, leading to a comprehensive and thorough review of child deaths in penal custody in England and Wales co-ordinated by an independent 'Standing Commission'. We intend that this, in turn, will be integrated within a wide and ambitious programme of policy reform that will ultimately deliver the abolition of the use of Prison Service and Private Sector custody for children. Ultimately, only this will lay the past to rest and mark real and meaningful progress towards a more humane, responsible and safer society.

Bibliography

Allen, R. (1991) 'Out of Jail: The reduction in the use of penal custody for male juveniles 1981-1988', *The Howard Journal of Criminal Justice*, Vol. 30 No. 1, pp. 30-52.

Ashton, J. and Grindrod, M. (1999) 'Institutional Troubleshooting: Lessons for Policy and Practice', in Goldson, B. (ed.) *Youth Justice: Contemporary Policy and Practice*, Aldershot, Ashgate, pp. 170-190.

Association of Directors of Social Services, Local Government Association, Youth Justice Board for England and Wales (2003) *The Application of the Children Act (1989) to Children in Young Offender Institutions*, London, ADSS, LGA and YJB.

Audit Commission (2004) 'Youth justice 2004: A review of the reformed youth justice system', *Criminal Justice Briefing*, London, Audit Commission.

Bateman, T. (2002) 'A Note on the Relationship between the Detention and Training Order and Section 91 of the Powers of the Criminal Courts (Sentencing) Act 2000: A Recipe for Injustice', *Youth Justice*, Vol. 1 No. 3, pp. 36-41.

Bateman, T. (2004a) 'Vulnerable children routinely held in prison service custody', Youth Justice News, *Youth Justice*, Vol. 4 No. 2, pp. 144-45.

Bateman, T. (2004b) 'Concern Over Restraint Procedures Following Death at Rainsbrook Secure Training Centre', Youth Justice News, *Youth Justice*, Vol. 4 No. 2, p. 143.

Bawdon, F. (2003) 'Dead Reckoning', *Independent Lawyer*, Issue 8, pp. 6-7.

Bishop, M. (2004) 'Coroners' Law Resource', http://www.kcl.ac.uk/depsta/law/research/coroners/middleton_sacker.html, site visited June 1, 2005.

British Broadcasting Corporation (2005) 'Prison numbers continue to climb', *BBC News Friday 27th May*, http://news.bbc.co.uk/1/hi/uk/4586949.stm

Beckett, C. (1999) 'Deaths in Custody and the Inquest System', *Critical Social Policy*, Vol. 19 No. 2, pp. 271-280.

Bennett, R. (2004) 'The human cost of zero tolerance', *The Guardian* G2, October 11, pp. 1-5.

Bowling, B. and Phillips, C. (2002) *Racism, Crime and Justice*, Harlow, Pearson.

Branigan, T. (2004) 'Mother of hanged boy, 14, warned jail of suicide risk', *The Guardian*, August 11.

British Medical Association (2001) *Prison Medicine: A Crisis Waiting to Break*, London, British Medical Association.

Challen, M. and Walton, T. (2004) *Juveniles in Custody*, London, Her Majesty's Inspectorate of Prisons.

Children's Rights Alliance for England (2002) *Rethinking child imprisonment: A report on young offender institutions*, London, Children's Rights Alliance for England.

Children's Society Advisory Committee on Juvenile Custody and its Alternatives (1993) *A False Sense of Security: The case against locking up more children*, London, The Children's Society.

Cohen, S. (1985) *Visions of Social Control*, Cambridge, Polity Press.

Cohen, S. (2001) *States of Denial: Knowing About Atrocities and Suffering*, Cambridge, Polity Press.

Coles, D. and Shaw, H. (2002) *How the inquest system fails bereaved people*, INQUEST'S Response to a Consultation Paper by the Fundamental Review of Death Certification and the Coroner Services in England, Wales and Northern Ireland, London, INQUEST.

Coles, D. and Shaw, H. (forthcoming, 2005) *Families Experiences Following Contentious Deaths in Custody*, London, INQUEST.

Coles, D. and Ward, T. (1994) 'Failure stories: Prison suicides and how not to prevent them', in Liebling, A. (ed.) *Deaths in Custody: International Perspectives*, London, Whiting and Birch, pp. 127-142.

Conservative Party (2005) *Are you thinking what we're thinking? It's time for action: Conservative Election Manifesto*, London, Conservative Party.

Corby, B., Doig, A. and Roberts, V. (2001) *Public Inquiries into Abuse of Children in Residential Care*, London, Jessica Kingsley.

Coulsfield, Lord (2004) *Crime, Courts and Confidence: Report of an independent inquiry into alternatives to prison*, London, Esmee Fairbairn Foundation.

Councell, R. (2003) *The prison population in 2002: a statistical review*, Findings 228, London, Home Office.

Councell, R. and Simes, J. (2002) *Projections of Long Term Trends in the Prison Population to 2009*, London, Home Office.

Cowan, R. (2005) 'Juvenile jail staff accused of racism', *The Guardian*, June 14.

Cragg, S. (2004) 'Middleton and Sacker: major development in inquest law', in *Inquest Law: Journal of the Inquest Lawyers Group*, May, pp. 1-3.

Dalrymple, J. (2001) *Secure Accommodation, YJB (01)57*, !2 September 2001, unpublished.

Davis, G., Lindsey, R., Seabourne, G. and Griffiths-Baker, J. (2002) *Experiencing inquests*, Home Office Research Study 241, London, Home Office Research, Development and Statistics Directorate.

Davis, H. and Bourhill, M. (1997) ' 'Crisis': The Demonisation of Children and Young People', in Scraton, P. (ed.) *'Childhood' in 'Crisis'?*, London, UCL Press, pp. 28-57.

Department of Constitutional Affairs (2004) *Notice of Consultation of Proposed Amendments to Guidance on the Public Funding of Legal Representation at Inquests Under Section 6 (8)(B) of the Access to Justice Act 1999*, London, Department of Constitutional Affairs.

Department for Education and Skills (2004) 'Safeguarding and promoting the welfare of children and young people in custody', *Local Authority Circular LAC (2004)26*, London, Department for Education and Skills.

Department of Health, Home Office and Department for Education and Employment (1999) *Working Together to Safeguard Children*, London, The Stationery Office.

Department of Health (2004) 'Memorandum from the Department of Health', written evidence to the House of Lords House of Commons Joint Committee on Human Rights *Deaths in Custody Interim Report: First Report of Session 2003-04*, London, The Stationery Office, Evidence 14-26.

Dodd, T., Nicholas, S., Povery, D. and Walker, A. (2004) *Crime in England and Wales 2003/2004*, Home Office Statistical Bulletin 10/04, London, Home Office.

Dooley, E. (1990) 'Prison Suicide in England and Wales, 1972-1987', *British Journal of Psychiatry*, Vol. 156, pp. 40-45.

Doughty Street Chambers (2004) 'Memorandum from Doughty Street Chambers', House of Lords House of Commons Joint Committee on Human Rights *Deaths in Custody Interim Report: First Report of Session 2003-04*, London, The Stationery Office, Evidence 85-87.

Dyer, C. (2005) 'Action pledged on coroners' system', *The Guardian*, May 18.

Farrant, F. (2001) *Troubled Inside: Responding to the Mental Health Needs of Children and Young People in Prison*, London, Prison Reform Trust.

Farrington, D., Hancock, G., Livingston, M., Painter, K. and Towl, G. (2000) *Evaluation of Intensive Regimes for Young Offenders*, Research Findings No. 21, London, Home Office.

Feilzer, M. and Hood, R. (2004) *Differences or Discrimination?*, London, Youth Justice Board for England and Wales.

Garland, D. (2001) *The Culture of Control*, Oxford, Oxford University Press.

Glasgow Media Group (2001) *Reporting Child Deaths: The Role of the Media*, London, National Association for the Prevention of Cruelty to Children.

Goldson, B. (1995) *A Sense of Security*, London, National Children's Bureau.

Goldson, B. (1997a) 'Children in Trouble: State Responses to Juvenile Crime', in Scraton, P. (ed.) *'Childhood' in 'Crisis'?*, London, UCL Press, pp. 124-145.

Goldson, B. (1997b) 'Children, Crime, Policy and Practice: Neither Welfare nor Justice', *Children and Society* Vol. 11 No. 2, pp. 77-88.

Goldson, B. (2000) ''Children in Need' or 'Young Offenders'? Hardening ideology, organisational change and new challenges for social work with children in trouble', *Child and Family Social Work* Vol, 5 No,.3, pp. 255-265.

Goldson, B. (2001a) 'Behind locked doors: Youth custody in crisis?', *Childright*, No 173, pp. 18-19.

Goldson, B (2001b) 'A Rational Youth Justice? Some Critical Reflections on the Research, Policy and Practice Relation', *Probation Journal* Vol. 48 No. 2, pp. 76-85.

Goldson, B. (2002a) 'New Punitiveness: The politics of child incarceration', in Muncie, J., Hughes, G. and McLaughlin, E. (eds.) *Youth Justice: Critical Readings*, London, Sage, pp. 386-400.

Goldson, B. (2002b) *Vulnerable Inside: Children in secure and penal settings*, London, The Children's Society.

Goldson, B. (2004a) 'Victims or Threats? Children, Care and Control', in Fink, J. (ed.) *Care: Personal Lives and Social Policy*, Bristol, The Policy Press in association with The Open University, pp. 77-109.

Goldson, B. (2004b) 'Youth Crime and Youth Justice', in Muncie, J. and Wilson, D. (eds.) *The Student Handbook of Criminal Justice and Criminology*, London, Cavendish Publishing, pp. 221-234.

Goldson, B. and Chigwada-Bailey, R. (1999) '(What) Justice for Black Children and Young People?', in Goldson, B. (ed.) *Youth Justice: Contemporary Policy and Practice*, Aldershot, Ashgate, pp. 51-74.

Graham, J. and Bowling, B. (1995) *Young people and crime*, Research Study 145, London, Home Office.

Graham, J. and Moore, C. (2004) *Trend Report on Juvenile Justice in England and Wales*, European Society of Criminology Thematic Group on Juvenile Justice, http://www.esc-eurocrim.org/workgroups.shtml#juvenile_justice, site visited August 24, 2004.

Hagell, A. and Hazel, N. (2001) 'Macro and Micro Patterns in the Development of Secure Custodial Institutions for Serious and Persistent Young Offenders in England and Wales', *Youth Justice*, Vol. 1 No. 1, pp. 3-16.

Harrington, V. and Mayhew, P. (2001) *Mobile Phone Theft*, Home Office Research Study 235, London, Home Office.

Hay, C. (1995) 'Mobilisation through interpellation: James Bulger, juvenile crime and the construction of a moral panic', *Social and Legal Studies*, Vol. 4 No. 2, pp. 197-223.

Haydon, D. and Scraton, P. (2000) 'Condemn a Little More, Understand a Little Less? The Political Context and Rights Implications of the Domestic and European Rulings in the Venables-Thompson Case', *Journal of Law and Society*, Vol. 27 No. 3, pp. 416-448.

Hazel, N., Hagell, A., Liddle, M., Archer, D., Grimshaw, R. and King, J. (2002) *Detention and Training: Assessment of the Detention and Training Order and its Impact on the Secure Estate across England and Wales*, London, Youth Justice Board for England and Wales.

Hentig, H. von (1937) *Punishment: Its Origins, Purpose and Psychology*, London, Hodge.

Her Majesty's Chief Inspector of Prisons (1990) *Review of Suicide and Self-Harm in Prison*, London, HMSO.

Her Majesty's Chief Inspector of Prisons (1997) *Young Prisoners: A Thematic Review by HM Chief Inspector of Prisons for England and Wales*, London, Home Office.

Her Majesty's Chief Inspector of Prisons (1999a) *Report on an Announced Inspection of HMP YOI Portland 24 October-3 November 1999 by HM Chief Inspector of Prisons*, London, Home Office.

Her Majesty's Chief Inspector of Prisons (1999b) *Suicide is Everyone's Concern: A Thematic Review by HM Chief Inspector of Prisons for England and Wales*, London, Home Office.

Her Majesty's Chief Inspector of Prisons (2001) *Report of Her Majesty's Chief Inspector of Prisons December 1999-November 2000*, London, Home Office.

Her Majesty's Chief Inspector of Prisons (2002a) *Annual Report of HM Chief Inspector of Prisons for England and Wales*, 2001-2002, London, The Stationery Office.

Her Majesty's Chief Inspector of Prisons (2002b) *Report on a Full Announced Inspection of HMYOI Feltham 14-23 January 2002 by HM Chief Inspector of Prisons*, London, Home Office.

Her Majesty's Chief Inspector of Prisons (2002c) *Report on a Full Announced Inspection of HMYOI Werrington 11-15 March 2002 by HM Chief Inspector of Prisons*, London, Home Office.

Her Majesty's Chief Inspector of Prisons (2003a) *Report on a Full Announced Inspection of HM Young Offender Institution Onley 27-31 January 2003 by HM Chief Inspector of Prisons*, London, Home Office.

Her Majesty's Chief Inspector of Prisons (2003b) *Report on a Full Announced Inspection of HM Young Offender Institution Castington 2-6 June 2003 by HM Chief Inspector of Prisons*, London, Home Office.

Her Majesty's Chief Inspector of Prisons (2003c) *Report on a Full Announced Inspection of HM Young Offender Institution Huntercombe 23-27 June 2003 by HM Chief Inspector of Prisons*, London, Home Office.

Her Majesty's Chief Inspector of Prisons (2004a) *Report on an Announced Inspection of HMP Eastwood Park 22-26 September 2003 by HM Chief Inspector of Prisons*, London, Home Office.

Her Majesty's Chief Inspector of Prisons (2004b) *Annual Report of HM Chief Inspector of Prisons for England and Wales, 2002-2003*, London, The Stationery Office.

Her Majesty's Chief Inspector of Prisons (2005) *Annual Report of HM Chief Inspector of Prisons for England and Wales, 2003-2004*, London, The Stationery Office.

Her Majesty's Chief Inspector of Prisons and The Office for Standards in Education (2001) *A Second Chance: A review of education and supporting arrangements within units for juveniles managed by HM Prison Service*, London, Home Office.

Her Majesty's Inspectorate of Prisons (2000) *Unjust deserts: A Thematic Review by HM Chief Inspector of Prisons of the Treatment and Conditions for Unsentenced Prisoners in England and Wales*, London, Her Majesty's Inspectorate of Prisons for England and Wales.

Her Majesty's Prison Service (2003) *Prison Service Order 4950: Regimes for Under 18 year Olds*, London, Her Majesty's Prison Service.

Her Majesty's Prison Service (2004) 'Memorandum from HM Prison Service', written evidence to the House of Lords House of Commons Joint Committee on Human Rights *Deaths in Custody Interim Report: First Report of Session 2003-04*, London, The Stationery Office, Evidence 26-32.

Her Majesty's Prison Service and the Youth Justice Board for England and Wales (2003) 'Child Protection and Safeguards Review 2003 – Draft', London, Her Majesty's Prison Service.

Holmes, C. and Gibbs, K. (2004) *Perceptions of Safety: Views of young people and staff living and working in the Juvenile Estate*, London, Her Majesty's Prison Service.

Home Office (1971) *Report on Death Certification and Coroners*, Cmnd 4810, London, HMSO.

Home Office (1984) *Suicide in Prisons: Report by Her Majesty's Chief Inspector of Prisons*, London, HMSO.

Home Office (1985) *The Cautioning of Offenders, Circular 14/1985*, London, Home Office.

Home Office (1988) *Punishment, Custody and the Community*, Cm 424, London, HMSO.

Home Office (1990) *The Cautioning of Offenders, Circular 59/90*, London, Home Office.

Home Office (2002) *Criminal Statistics for England and Wales 2001*, London, Home Office.

Home Office (2003a) *Prison statistics England and Wales*, London, The Stationery Office.

Home Office (2003b) *World Prison Population List*, Findings 234, London, Home Office.

Home Office (2003c) *Death Certification and Investigation in England, Wales and Northern Ireland: The Report of a Fundamental Review 2003*, London, The Stationery Office.

Home Office (2003d) *Prisons and Probation Ombudsman: Framework for a statutory complaints procedure and procedure for investigating deaths in prison custody and of approved premises' residents*, London, The Home Office.

Home Office (2004a) *Race and the Criminal Justice System: An overview to the complete statistics 2002-03*, London, Home Office.

Home Office (2004b) 'Prisons and Probation Ombudsman to Investigate all Prison Deaths', *Home Office Press Release*, 6 January, London, Home Office.

Home Office (2004c) *Reforming the Coroner and Death Certification Service: A Position paper*, London, The Stationery Office.

Hough, M., Jacobson, J. and Millie, A. (2003) *The Decision to Imprison: Key Findings*, London, Prison Reform Trust.

House of Commons (2005) 'Government Bills 2005/06 – in progress', http://commonsleader.gov.uk/textonly/Page946.asp, site visited June 1, 2005.

House of Commons Committee of Public Accounts (2004) *Youth offending: the delivery of community and custodial sentences*: Fortieth Report of Session 2003-04, London, The Stationery Office.

House of Lords House of Commons Joint Committee on Human Rights (2003) *The UN Convention on the Rights of the Child: Tenth Report of Session 2002-03*, London, The Stationery Office.

House of Lords House of Commons Joint Committee on Human Rights (2004a) *Deaths in Custody Interim Report: First Report of Session 2003-04*, London, The Stationery Office.

House of Lords House of Commons Joint Committee on Human Rights (2004b) *Deaths in Custody: Third Report of Session 2004-05*, London, The Stationery Office.

House of Lords House of Commons Joint Committee on Human Rights (2005) *Government Response to the Third Report from the Committee: Deaths in Custody: Eleventh Report of Session 2004-05*, London, The Stationery Office.

Howard League for Penal Reform (1993a) *Suicides in Feltham*, London, The Howard League for Penal Reform.

Howard League for Penal Reform (1993b) *Dying inside: Suicides in Prison*, London, The Howard League for Penal Reform.

Howard League for Penal Reform (1995) *Secure Training Centres: repeating past failures*, Briefing Paper, London, The Howard League for Penal Reform.

Howard League for Penal Reform (1999) *Desperate Measures: prison suicides and their prevention*, London, The Howard League for Penal Reform.

Howard League for Penal Reform (2001a) *Children in prison: provision and practice at Castington*. London, The Howard League for Penal Reform.

Howard League for Penal Reform (2001b) *Suicide and Self-Harm Prevention: Repetitive self-harm among women and girls in prison*, London, The Howard League for Penal Reform

Howard League for Penal Reform (2004a) *Prison Overcrowding: 75,000 behind bars*, Briefing Paper, London, The Howard League for Penal Reform.

Howard League for Penal Reform (2004b) 'Girls held in adult prisons against their "best interests"', *Press Release 20 January*, London, The Howard League for Penal Reform.

Howard League for Penal Reform (2005) *Children in custody: promoting the legal and human rights of children*, London, The Howard League for Penal Reform.

Howe, L. (2004) 'Memorandum from Dr Leonie Howe', written evidence to the House of Lords House of Commons Joint Committee on Human Rights *Deaths in Custody Interim Report: First Report of Session 2003-04*, London, The Stationery Office, Evidence 118-129.

Hughes, R. and Thompson, B. (2000) 'Under 18 year olds: Making the Difference', *Prison Service Journal*, No. 128, pp. 4-7.

INQUEST (1990) *Annual Report 1989-1990*, London, INQUEST.

INQUEST (1992) *Annual Report 1991-1992*, London, INQUEST.

INQUEST (1993) *Annual Report 1992-1993*, London, INQUEST.

INQUEST (1994) *Annual Report 1994*, London, INQUEST.

INQUEST (1996) *Annual Report 1995/96*, London, INQUEST.

INQUEST (1999) *Annual Report 1999*, London, INQUEST.

INQUEST (2000) *Annual Report 2000*, London, INQUEST.

INQUEST (2001) *Annual Report 2001*, London, INQUEST.

INQUEST (2002) 'Inquest opens into death of 16 year old in Feltham Young Offender Institution 11th September 2002', *Press Release*, September, London, INQUEST.

INQUEST (2003a) *Annual Report 2003*, London, INQUEST.

INQUEST (2003b) *Deaths in Custody – the current issues: A submission to the Joint Committee on Human Rights – Inquiry into deaths in custody*, December 2003, London, INQUEST.

INQUEST (2004a) *Annual Report 2004*, London, INQUEST.

INQUEST (2004b) 'Memorandum from Inquest', House of Lords House of Commons Joint Committee on Human Rights *Deaths in Custody Interim Report: First Report of Session 2003-04*, London, The Stationery Office, Evidence 88-101.

INQUEST (2004c) *INQUEST's further evidence to the Joint Committee on Human Rights September 2004: Deaths in Custody – The Current Issues*, London, INQUEST.

INQUEST (2005a) 'Deaths in Prison', http://inquest.gn.apc.org/ stats_prison.html, site visited March 11, 2005.

INQUEST (2005b) 'Personal Communication with the Prison Service's Safer Custody Group', May 27.

INQUEST and Nacro (2003) *A child's death in custody: Call for a public inquiry.* London, INQUEST and Nacro.

INQUEST and Nacro (2004) *Why are children dying in custody? Call for a public inquiry into the death of Joseph Scholes.* London, INQUEST and Nacro.

Jenks, C. (1996) *Childhood*, London, Routledge.

Jerrom, C. (2004) 'Death without Respect', *Community Care*, 16-22 September, pp. 30-33.

Kahan. B. (1994) *Growing up in Groups*, London, HMSO.

Kennedy, H. (1995) 'Preface', *Banged up, Beaten up and Cutting up*, London, The Howard League for Penal Reform.

Labour Party (2005) *Britain forward not back: The Labour Party Manifesto*, London, The Labour Party.

Lader, D., Singleton, N. and Meltzer, H. (2000) *Psychiatric Morbidity among Young Offenders in England and Wales*, London, Office for National Statistics.

Leech, M. and Cheney, D. (2001) *The Prisons Handbook*, Winchester, Waterside Press.

Liberal Democratic Party (2004) 'Tough Liberalism', speech presented by Rt. Hon. Charles Kennedy, 30 March, 2004, http://www.libdems.org.uk/parliament/feature.html?id=6453, site visited April 29, 2005.

Liberty (2003) *Deaths in Custody: Redress and Remedies*, London, The Civil Liberties Trust.

Liberty (2004) 'Memorandum from Liberty', written evidence to the House of Lords House of Commons Joint Committee on Human Rights *Deaths in Custody Interim Report: First Report of Session 2003-04*, London, The Stationery Office, Evidence 102-106.

Liebling, A. (1996) 'Prison Suicides: What Progress Research?', in Liebling, A. (ed.) *Deaths in Custody: Caring for People at Risk*, London, Whiting and Birch, pp. 41-53.

Liebling, A. (1998) 'Prison Suicide and the Nature of Imprisonment', in Liebling, A. (ed.) *Deaths of Offenders: The Hidden Side of Justice*, Winchester, Waterside Press, pp. 64-74.

Liebling, A. (2004) 'Legitimacy, Distress and Prison Suicide', paper presented at the *Effects of Imprisonment International Symposium*, Robinson College, University of Cambridge, April 14-15, unpublished.

Liebling, A. and Krarup, H. (1993) *Suicide Attempts and Self-Injury in Male Prisons*. London, Home Office.

Lyon, J., Dennison, C., Wilson, A. (2000) *'Tell Them So They Listen': Messages from Young People in Custody*, London, Home Office.

Macpherson, Sir William (1999) *The Stephen Lawrence Inquiry: Report of an Inquiry by Sir William Macpherson of Cluny*, Cmnd 4262-1, London, The Stationery Office.

McHugh, M. and Snow, L. (2000) 'Suicide prevention: policy and practice', in Towl, G; Snow, L. and McHugh, M. (eds.) *Suicide in Prisons*, Leicester, British Psychological Society, pp. 1-25.

Medlicott, D. (2001) *Surviving the Prison Place: Narratives of Suicidal Prisoners*, Aldershot, Ashgate.

Mental Health Foundation (1999) *Bright Futures: Promoting Young People's Mental Health*, London, Salzburg-Wittenburg.

Miller, J. (1991) *Last One Over the Wall: The Massachusetts Experiment in Closing Reform Schools*, Ohio, Ohio State University Press.

Mills, A. (2004) 'Memorandum from Dr Alice Mills', written evidence to the House of Lords House of Commons Joint Committee on Human Rights *Deaths in Custody Interim Report: First Report of Session 2003-04*, London, The Stationery Office, Evidence 129-135.

Mind (2004) 'Memorandum submitted by Mind', written evidence to the House of Lords House of Commons Joint Committee on Human Rights

Deaths in Custody Interim Report: First Report of Session 2003-04, London, The Stationery Office, Evidence 107-113.

Monaghan, G., Hibbert, P. and Moore, S. (2003) *Children in trouble: Time for change,* London, Barnardo's.

Moore, P. and Taggart, T. (1991) 'The Glen Parva Experience', in INQUEST *Annual Report 1991,* London, INQUEST.

Moore, S. (2000) 'Child Incarceration and the New Youth Justice', in Goldson, B. (ed.) *The New Youth Justice,* Dorset, Russell House Publishing, pp. 115-128.

Morgan, R. (1996) 'In the hands of the state: Care and accountability', in Liebling, A. (ed.) *Deaths in Custody: Caring for People at Risk,* London, Whiting and Birch, pp. 6-27.

Morgan, R. (2004) 'Where does child welfare fit into youth justice', paper presented at *Children First, Offending Second?,* Nacro Youth Crime Conference, Loughborough University, April, unpublished.

Morris, N. (2004) 'Government's policy of privately run jails set to continue', *The Independent, 11 August.*

Munby, The Honourable Mr Justice (2002) *Judgment Approved by the Court for Handing Down in R (on the application of the Howard League for Penal Reform) v. The Secretary of State for the Home Department,* 29 November, London, Royal Courts of Justice.

Muncie, J. (1999) 'Institutionalised Intolerance: Youth Justice and the 1998 Crime and Disorder Act, *Critical Social Policy,* Vol. 19 No. 2, pp 147-175.

Muncie, J. (2003) *Juvenile justice in Europe: Some conceptual, analytical and statistical comparisons,* Childright, No. 202, pp. 14-17.

Muncie, J. (2004) *Youth and Crime,* London, Sage.

Muncie, J. (2005) 'The globalization of crime control – the case of youth and juvenile justice: Neo-liberalism, policy convergence and international conventions', in *Theoretical Criminology,* Volume 9 Number 1, pp. 35-64.

Muncie, J. and Goldson, B. (eds.) (forthcoming, 2006) *Comparative Juvenile Justice,* London, Sage.

Owen, T. and Friedman, D. (2002) 'Inquests and the Human Rights Act – The State's obligation to investigate deaths in custody: a summary of recent developments in case law', in *Inquest Law: Journal of the Inquest Lawyer's Group,* Spring issue, pp. 1-3.

Nacro (1988) 'Juveniles Remanded in Custody', *Nacro Briefing,* November, London, Nacro.

Nacro (1989a) *Phasing Out Prison Department Custody for Juvenile Offenders,* London, Nacro.

Nacro (1989b) *Replacing Custody: Findings from Two Census Surveys of Schemes for Juvenile Offenders Funded Under the DHSS Intermediate Treatment Initiative Covering the Period January to December 1987,* London, Nacro.

Nacro (1991) 'Juveniles Remanded in Custody', *Nacro Briefing,* September, London, Nacro.

Nacro (2000) *Unlocking potential: reducing the incarceration of children in England and Wales,* London, Nacro.

Nacro (2003) *A failure of justice: Reducing child imprisonment,* London, Nacro.

Nacro (2004a) *Youth Crime Briefing: New Legislation – impact on sentencing,* March, London, Nacro.

Nacro (2004b) *Youth Crime Briefing: Some facts about young people who offend – 2002,* March, London, Nacro.

Nacro (2005) *A better alternative: Reducing child imprisonment,* London, Nacro.

Nathan, S. (2000) 'Detention and Training Orders – Further Experimentation in Juvenile Incarceration', *Youth Justice Matters,* June 2000, pp. 3-11.

Neal, D. (1996) 'Prison Suicides: What Progress Policy and Practice?', in Liebling, A. (ed.) *Deaths in Custody: Caring for People at Risk,* London, Whiting and Birch, pp. 54-67.

Parliamentary Commission for Administration (1999) *7th Annual Report: Session 1998-9,* London, The Stationery Office.

Penal Affairs Consortium (1994)*The Case Against the Secure Training Order,* London, Penal Affairs Consortium.

Penal Affairs Consortium (1996) *Juveniles on Remand: Recent Trends in the Remanding of Juveniles to Prison Service Custody,* London, Penal Affairs Consortium.

Phillips, M. (1986) 'A Study of Suicide and Attempted Suicide at HMP Brixton', *Department of Psychological Services Report,* Series 1, 24, Prison Service, London.

Pitts, J. (2000) 'The New Youth Justice and the Politics of Electoral Anxiety', in Goldson, B. (ed.) *The New Youth Justice,* Dorset, Russell House Publishing, pp. 1-13.

Pratt, J., Brown, D., Brown, M., Hallsworth, S. and Morrison, W. (eds.) (2005) *The New Punitiveness: Trends, theories, perspectives,* Cullompton, Willan.

Press Association (2004) 'Review launched into child death tactics', www.guardian.co.uk/prisons/story/0,7369,1299063,00.html, site visited October 25, 2004.

Prisons and Probation Ombudsman for England and Wales (2004) 'Memorandum from Prisons and Probation Ombudsman for England and Wales', written evidence to the House of Lords House of Commons Joint Committee on Human Rights *Deaths in Custody Interim Report: First Report of Session 2003-04*, London, The Stationery Office, Evidence 67-68.

Prisons and Probation Ombudsman for England and Wales (2005) *Guidance on Disclosure*, London, Prisons and Probation Ombudsman for England and Wales.

Prison Reform Trust (2004a) *Prison Reform Trust Factfile: July 2004*, London, Prison Reform Trust.

Prison Reform Trust (2004b) 'Memorandum from the Prison Reform Trust', written evidence to the House of Lords House of Commons Joint Committee on Human Rights *Deaths in Custody Interim Report: First Report of Session 2003-04*, London, The Stationery Office, Evidence 113-117.

Round, V. (2004) 'Coroner Reform', http://www.kcl.ac.uk/depsta/law/research/coroners/ HOpositionpaper.html, site visited June 1, 2005.

Rutherford, A. (1995) 'Signposting the future of juvenile justice policy in England and Wales', in *Child Offenders: UK and International Practice*, London, The Howard League for Penal Reform.

Ryan. M. (1996) *'Lobbying From Below: INQUEST in defence of civil liberties*, London, UCL Press.

Scraton, P. (1999) *Hillsborough: The Truth*, Edinburgh, Mainstream Publishing.

Scraton, P. and Chadwick, K. (1986) '"The Experiment that Went Wrong": The Crisis of Death in Youth Custody at the Glenochil Complex', in Rolston, B. and Tomlinson, M. (eds.) *The Expansion of European Prison Systems: Working Papers in European Criminology No. 7*, Belfast, European Group for the Study of Deviance and Social Control, pp. 145-160.

Scraton, P. and Chadwick, K. (1987a) ' 'Speaking Ill of the Dead': Institutionalised Responses to Deaths in Custody', in Scraton, P. (ed.) *Law, Order and the Authoritarian State*, Milton Keynes, Open University Press, pp. 212-236.

Scraton, P. and Chadwick, K. (1987b) *In the Arms of the Law: Coroners' Inquests and Deaths in Custody*, London, Pluto.

Scraton, P., Jemphrey, A. and Coleman, S. (1995) *No Last Rights: The denial of justice and the creation of myth in the aftermath of the Hillsborough disaster*, Liverpool, Liverpool City Council.

Scraton, P. and Moore, L. (2004) *The Hurt Inside: The imprisonment of women and girls in Northern Ireland*, Belfast, Northern Ireland Human Rights Commission.

Secure Accommodation Network (2005) 'Directory of Units', http://www. secureaccommodation. net/unitlist2.htm, site visited May 5, 2005.

Sim, J. (1990) *Medical Power in Prisons: The Prison Medical Service in England 1774-1989*, Milton Keynes and Philadelphia, Open University Press.

Snow, L. and McHugh, M. (2000) 'The aftermath of a death in prison custody', in Towl, G., Snow, L. and McHugh, M. (eds.) *Suicide in Prisons*, Leicester, British Psychological Society, pp. 135-155.

Social Exclusion Unit (2002a) *Reducing re-offending by ex-prisoners*, London, Social Exclusion Unit.

Social Exclusion Unit (2002b) *Reducing re-offending by ex-prisoners: Summary of the Social Exclusion Unit Report*, London, Social Exclusion Unit.

Social Services Inspectorate, Commission for Health Improvement, Her Majesty's Chief Inspector of Constabulary, Her Majesty's Chief Inspector of the Crown Prosecution Service, Her Majesty's Chief Inspector of the Magistrates' Courts Service, Her Majesty's Chief Inspector of Schools, Her Majesty's Chief Inspector of Prisons and Her Majesty's Chief Inspector of Probation (2002) *Safeguarding Children: A joint Chief Inspectors' Report on Arrangements to Safeguard Children*, London, Department of Health Publications.

Stern, V. (1998) *A Sin Against the Future: Imprisonment in the World*, London, Penguin.

Stuart, M. and Baines, C. (2004) *Safeguards for vulnerable children: Three studies on abusers, disabled children and children in prison*, York, Joseph Rowntree Foundation.

Thomas, L., Friedman, D. and Christian, L. (2002) *Inquests: a practitioners guide*, London, Legal Action Group.

Topp, D. O. (1979) 'Suicide in Prison', *British Journal of Psychiatry*, Vol. 134, pp. 24-27.

Towl, G. and Crighton, D. (2000) 'Risk assessment and management', in Towl, G., Snow, L. and McHugh, M. (eds.) *Suicide in Prisons*, Leicester, British Psychological Society, pp. 66-92.

Travis, A. (2004) 'Jailed teenager died after being restrained', *The Guardian*, April 23, p. 7.

United Nations Committee on the Rights of the Child (2002) *Committee on the Rights of the Child Thirty First Session – Concluding Observations of the Committee on the Rights of the Child: United Kingdom of Great Britain and Northern Ireland*, Geneva, Office of the United Nations High Commissioner for Human Rights.

United Nations General Assembly (1989) *The United Nations Convention on the Rights of the Child*, New York, United Nations.

Utting, Sir W. (1997) *People Like Us: The Report of the Review of the Safeguards for Children Living Away from Home*, London, The Stationery Office.

Valier, C. (2004) 'Litigation as a Strategy in Penal Reform', *The Howard Journal of Criminal Justice*, Vol. 43 No. 1, pp. 15-26.

Webster, C. (forthcoming, 2006) ''Race', Youth Crime and Justice', in Goldson, B. and Muncie, J. (eds.) *Youth Crime and Justice*, London, Sage.

Wilson, D. (2004) ''Keeping Quiet' or 'Going Nuts': Strategies Used by Young, Black, Men in Custody', *The Howard Journal of Criminal Justice*, Vol. 43 No. 3, pp. 317-330.

Worrall, A. (1999) 'Troubled or Troublesome? Justice for Girls and Young Women', in Goldson, B. (ed.) *Youth Justice: Contemporary Policy and Practice*, Aldershot, Ashgate, pp. 28-50.

Youth Justice Board for England and Wales (1998) *Juvenile Secure Estate: Preliminary Advice from the Youth Justice Board for England and Wales to the Home Secretary*, London, Youth Justice Board for England and Wales.

Youth Justice Board for England and Wales (2000a) *National Standards for Youth Justice*, London, Youth Justice Board for England and Wales.

Youth Justice Board for England and Wales (2000b) *Youth Justice Board News*, Issue 4, London, Youth Justice Board for England and Wales.

Youth Justice Board for England and Wales (2000c) *Secure Facilities Placement System*, Circular to YOT Managers, Local Authority Secure Unit Managers, YOI Governors and Secure Training Centre Managers, 16 October, London, Youth Justice Board for England and Wales.

Youth Justice Board for England and Wales (2001) *T1:V – Initial Custodial Reception Assessment – Guidance for Completion*, London, Youth Justice Board for England and Wales.

Youth Justice Board for England and Wales (2003) *Gaining Ground in the Community: Youth Justice Board Annual Review 2002-03*, London, Youth Justice Board for England and Wales.

Youth Justice Board for England and Wales (2004a) *Strategy for the Secure Estate for Juveniles: Building on the foundations*, London, Youth Justice Board for England and Wales.

Youth Justice Board for England and Wales (2004b) *National Standards for Youth Justice*, London, Youth Justice Board for England and Wales.

Youth Justice Board for England and Wales (2004c) *Secure Facilities – Placement Policy*, November, London, Youth Justice Board for England and Wales.

Youth Justice Board for England and Wales (2004d) *Secure Facilities – Placement Protocol*, November, London, Youth Justice Board for England and Wales.

Youth Justice Board for England and Wales (2005) *Youth Justice Annual Statistics 2003/04*, London, Youth Justice Board for England and Wales.

Index

Inquest Charitable Trust (known as INQUEST) provides a specialist, comprehensive advice service to bereaved people, lawyers, other advice and support agencies, the media, MPs and the wider public on contentious deaths and their investigation, and all aspects of the inquest system. INQUEST was established in 1981 following a number of controversial deaths in police and prison custody. Deaths in custody remain the main focus of INQUEST's work.

INQUEST has a free information pack for *any* bereaved family that explains the inquest process and where to find emotional and practical support. The organisation provides an in-depth casework service to the families of people who have died in detention (police custody, prison, immigration and psychiatric detention). The focus on deaths in custody and the monitoring of such deaths means that the organisation is at the forefront of uncovering patterns and trends in this area.

Through its casework and monitoring the organisation develops policy proposals and undertakes research to lobby for changes to the inquest and investigation process, to reduce the number of custodial deaths and to improve the treatment and care of those within the institutions where the deaths occur.

Working for truth, justice and accountability

89-93 Fonthill Road, London N4 3JH, UK
Tel: 020 7263 1111 Fax: 020 7561 0799
Email: inquest@inquest.org.uk
Website: www.inquest.org.uk
Registered charity number 1046650
Company number 03054853

Diana

THE WORK CONTINUES